Columbus, Indiana
A Look At Modern Architecture & Art

8th Edition

This edition is dedicated to:

J. Irwin Miller (1909-2004)
Xenia S. Miller (1908-2008)
The Citizens of Columbus

*for their commitment to design excellence
and the quality of life of their community.*

Copyright 1974, 1980, 1982, 1984, 1991, 1998, 2012
All rights reserved: Columbus Area Visitors Center and Steven R. Risting
Published by Columbus Area Visitors Center, Columbus, Indiana
Eighth Edition

ISBN: 978-0-615-74469-8
1. Columbus, Indiana
2. Architecture - United States - 21st century
3. Art - United States - public

Every effort has been made to make this book as accurate as possible.
Any errors or omissions are not intentional. This book should serve only
as a general guide and not as the ultimate source of the subject information.
The editor, publisher and the Columbus Area Visitors Center shall have
no liability or responsibility to any person or entity regarding any loss or
damage incurred, or alleged to have incurred, directly or indirectly,
by the information contained in this book.

Table of Contents

	Page
Forward	5
Introduction	7
J. Irwin Miller and Cummins Commitment	9
A Commitment to Downtown Columbus	11
National Recognition of Columbus, Indiana	13
Connections, Collaboration, Community	17
A Look at Modern Architecture in Columbus, Indiana	19
Public Art in Columbus, Indiana	167
Historic Architecture in Columbus, Indiana	199
Appendix	213

    TIMELINE of selected Architecture, Landscape Architecture and Art
    Architects / Landscape Architects / Artists and their works in Columbus, IN
    Modern Architecture and Public Art listed alphabetically with location
    Columbus, Indiana Contractors contribution to excellence
    Columbus, Indiana MAP
    Acknowledgements / Credits

Forward

Columbus is a small southern Indiana community internationally recognized for its modern architecture and art. Through the patronage of J. Irwin Miller, Cummins, and many other community leaders and companies, Columbus has transformed itself from just another Midwestern town to a community culturally enriched by modern design.

The Visitors Center of Columbus first published this book in 1974, recognizing over 40 modern buildings and major sculptures that had been completed in Columbus since 1942. The last edition of this book published in 1998 recognized over 66 modern buildings, projects and major sculptures. In the last 14 years Columbus has continued its commitment to design excellence, with over 15 new buildings, many associated with the downtown redevelopment. Columbus garnered national attention in 2011 with the opening of the Miller House and Garden for public tours.

This eighth edition guidebook presents new color photographs of the major modern buildings, public art and significant historic buildings as they currently exist. The first seven book editions featured a single black and white building photographed by Balthazar Korab, originally an architect in Eero Saarinen's office. Steven Risting, an Indianapolis architect leading or collaborating on the design of several of the recent Columbus projects, has photographed with an architect's eye how the buildings and artwork relate to their surroundings, with additional images of interior space and architectural details. He has further researched each building to not only recognize the lead architectural designer, but to also give credit to design collaborators and local associations. In addition he has highlighted either the architect's design concept or the client's design intent, to show a more personal connection between the designers and the projects they created for Columbus. This book has also been reorganized, with a separate section on public art.

Whether you are an architect or artist, architectural buff or just interested in good design, we believe you will find Columbus, Indiana unexpected and unforgettable.

                    Lynn Lucas
                    Executive Director
                    Columbus Area Visitors Center
                    2012

The Commons and Bartholomew County Courthouse (*photo by Susan Fleck*)

Introduction

Columbus, Indiana is the county seat of Bartholomew County, with a growing population of almost 12,000 people in 1940 to over 44,000 in 2010. Located south of Indianapolis, it lies between the convergence of two rivers. Downtown Columbus features an 1874 second-empire styled courthouse building, located on a traditional open courthouse square. Washington Street is the "main" street, predominantly framed with Victorian commercial buildings and storefronts.

The town's development and community growth was fostered by the arrival of the railroads in the mid-1840s. Joseph Ireland Irwin established a general store in 1850, which began a business dynasty that grew to include banking, agricultural milling, transportation networks and a philanthropic foundation. His son William G. Irwin, invested in Cummins Engine Company (Cummins, Inc.), founded by his family's chauffeur Clessie Cummins in 1919, and his grandnephew J. Irwin Miller joined the struggling company in 1934. J. Irwin Miller ultimately led Cummins to its status as an international leader in the manufacturing of diesel engines. Columbus is also home to many other manufacturing companies.

The Irwin family and its extended clan of Sweeney's and Miller's have made an enormous impact on the quality of living and architectural character of Columbus. In 1942, the parishioners of Tabernacle Church of Christ, including William G. Irwin and his sister Linnie I. Sweeney, wife of Rev. Sweeney, commissioned Eliel Saarinen to design a modern church, recognized as one of the first churches of contemporary architecture in the United States. In 1955, Columbus received further national recognition for its modern architecture as "the envy of any small town in the U.S." for the recently completed low glass pavilion of Irwin Union Bank on Washington Street designed by Eero Saarinen.

Community leaders embraced the strategy to design modern buildings to create a better community, and one that could attract and retain bright, talented individuals and their families to this small southern Indiana town. While many of the buildings were designed by architects early in their careers, many of these architects and artists are now nationally and internationally renowned, including Eliel Saarinen, Eero Saarinen, Harry Weese, Gunnar Birkerts, Robert Venturi, I.M. Pei, Kevin Roche, Cesar Pelli, Richard Meier, Henry Moore, Jean Tinguely, and Dale Chihuly.

Most of downtown Columbus is listed on the National Register of Historic Places. In 2000, in a highly unusual move, six modern buildings and landscapes in Columbus were simultaneously designated as National Historic Landmarks by the National Park Service, part of the United States Department of the Interior. They were cited as important works in the development of modernism in architecture and landscape architecture and possess national significance in commemorating the history of the United States of America. These Historic Landmarks include First Christian Church, Irwin Union Bank, the Miller House and Garden, Mabel McDowell School, North Christian Church, and First Baptist Church. In 2012, The Republic became the seventh designated Historic Landmark site.

While much of the focus on Columbus is on its architecture and art, the strategy underlying this commitment has succeeded in creating a higher quality of life for the entire community, as recognized in a number of national rankings: "top 100 places to live in America", "top 100 Best Communities of Young People", "top 10 affordable cities for retirement", 4th for quality of life in a small city of 10,000-50,000, one of the "most walkable" communities in America, one of the Ten Most Playful Towns in America, one of the country's safest metropolitan areas, and "Best of the Best" for landscape design. The community has also won national awards for sports events, the America in Bloom national competition for cities with a population between 25,000-50,000, and national awards for its park and trail system. National Geographic Traveler 2008 ranked Columbus 11th out of 109 worldwide historic distinctions. Richard Florida, author of The Rise of the Creative Class, noted that "Columbus is a creative community that truly gets it."

No one will call a community "good," unless it looks like a "good" community. By American tradition, a good city must be defined as one which provides the "good things" for all its residents - schools, parks, churches, civic buildings, programs that meet community needs, and events that entertain. Living in Columbus means caring about making the community a better place to live. There is a commitment to save the best of the old and build for the future in a quality way that everyone will consider worth saving.

Otto Creek Golf Course and Clubhouse

J. Irwin Miller and Cummins Commitment

While not all of the modern buildings constructed in Columbus, Indiana were designed by prominent architects supported by the Cummins Foundation Architecture Program, many are connected to the humble influence and the commitment to design excellence by J. Irwin Miller and Cummins.

In 1939, J. Irwin Miller was influential is convincing Eliel Saarinen to design a contemporary church in Columbus. During the design process of First Christian Church, Mr. Miller became close friends with Eliel's son Eero Saarinen. They would often meet at the downtown Zaharako's Ice Cream Parlor to discuss architecture, philosophy and their many plans for the future.

As the president and chairman of the Cummins Engine Company, and head of the Irwin Union Bank, Mr. Miller hired Eero Saarinen in 1950 to design the downtown bank and in 1953 to design his home, as well as in 1959 to design North Christian Church. In the early 1950s, as a member of a mayor's committee to build new rental housing that could be used as an incentive to attract the brightest and most capable young people, many from Ivy League schools, to a small Midwestern town, Mr. Miller interviewed Harry Weese who was recommended by Eero Saarinen, to design Columbus Village, phase one completed in 1954. Harry Weese would become a close friend, designing over 18 buildings in Columbus, not only for Cummins and the bank, but also for private residences, schools, the Salvation Army, another local manufacturing company, an ice rink and First Baptist Church.

In 1957, Mr. Miller offered a unique proposal to the local school board. Cummins Engine Foundation (renamed The Cummins Foundation) would pay for the architect's fees, with the stipulation that the school board would select an architect from a list of prominent architects provided by the Foundation. It was the responsibility of the school board to make the final selection, without the further involvement of the Foundation, and to pay for all the construction costs. After the initial success of this proposal at Schmitt Elementary School designed by Harry Weese and several other schools, the Cummins Foundation Architecture Program was eventually created and expanded to be available to public buildings in Bartholomew County.

J. Irwin Miller's and Cummins' commitment to Columbus is summarized in his remarks for the dedication of Otter Creek Clubhouse and Golf Course on June 21, 1964.

"Why should an industrial company, organized for profit, think it a good and right thing to take a million dollars, and more, of that profit, and give it to this community in the form of this golf course and clubhouse? Why, instead, isn't Cummins - the largest taxpayer in the county, spending the same energy to try to get its taxes reduced, the cost of education cut, the cost of city government cut, less money spent on streets and utilities and schools?

"This answer is that we would like to see the community come to be not the cheapest community in America, but the very best community of its size in the country. We would like to see it become the city in which the smartest, the ablest, the best young families anywhere would like to live…a community that is open in every single respect to persons of every race, color and opinion; that makes them feel welcome and at home…a community which will offer their children the best education available anywhere… a community of strong, outspoken churches, of genuine cultural interests, exciting opportunities for recreation…a community whose citizens are themselves well paid and who will not tolerate poverty for others, or slums in their midst.

"No such community can be built without citizens determined to make their community best; without city government which works boldly – ahead of its problems, and not always struggling to catch up - and without money sufficient to get the job done.

"So Cummins is not for cheap education, or inadequate, poorly-paid government, or second-rate facilities or low taxes just for the sake of low taxes. Our concern is to help get the most for our dollar, to help build this community into the best in the nation. And we are happy to pay our share, whether in work, or in taxes, or in gifts like this one."

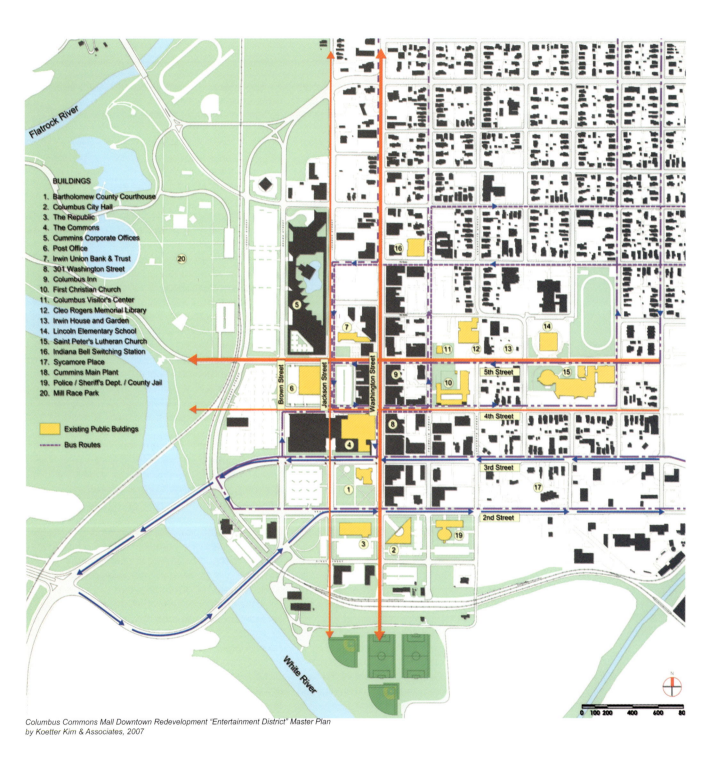

*Columbus Commons Mall Downtown Redevelopment "Entertainment District" Master Plan
by Koetter Kim & Associates, 2007*

A Commitment to Downtown Columbus

The downtown is the central element of a healthy, growing community. Columbus has been committed to maintaining and enhancing the quality of its downtown, as exemplified by numerous studies, projects, preservation of historic buildings, and the intervention of many modern buildings.

In the 1960s, with people moving to the suburbs, the Columbus Redevelopment Commission was formed. Ideas to "brighten up" and "re-awaken interest in downtown" were proposed by Alexander Girard in 1964, including painting the Victorian facades and suggesting new signage on Washington Street. In 1965, a redevelopment and urban renewal plan was created, including the removal of several buildings that were beyond repair, as well as specific development criteria.

A 1968 downtown master plan by Skidmore, Owings & Merrill (SOM) noted "…an aging center which has been unable to make a satisfactory adjustment to the changing economic conditions brought about by the impact of the automobile…" and recommended the creation of two retail "super blocks", one of which was realized in 1973 with The Commons and Commons Mall designed by Cesar Pelli. Tipton Lakes on the west side was also created at the same time, to re-centralize the population that had been expanding only to the north and east. Lincoln Elementary School by Gunnar Birkerts (1967) and the public library by I.M. Pei (1969), with a public plaza and a proposed conference center began to identify 5th Street as an architecturally significant street. The U.S. Post Office by Kevin Roche (1970), The Republic by SOM (1971), and the Irwin Union Bank office and arcade by Kevin Roche (1972) further enlivened downtown. Architectural tours of Columbus began in 1973 with the renovation of the historic Storey house by Bruce Adams as a Visitors Center.

Even with the construction of the AT&T Switching Center by Paul Kennon (1978) and the City Hall by SOM (1981), the recession of the late 1970s and early 1980s affected the livelihood of the downtown. In 1983 SOM created another Central Area Master Plan, "…to preserve and enhance the existing urban fabric of the community." Cummins' commitment to downtown was demonstrated with a three-block corporate office building designed by Kevin Roche, constructed north of 5th Street between Jackson and Brown Streets. St. Peter's Lutheran Church completed a new sanctuary in 1988 designed by Gunnar Birkerts.

In 1988, architect Paul Kennon was asked to extend his "squatters" concept to the field of urban design. With public interviews and dialogue, he made several proposals to make downtown more attractive, vital and active. These ideas included patterned brick intersections, donor brick sidewalks and new lighting which were implemented on Washington Street, as well as alleyways.

The national economic success of the 1990s saw proposals for the improvement of the entry into downtown from the interstate by Robert Venturi and Michael Van Valkenburgh, with the realization of a "Gateway Arch" Bridge in 1997 and the dramatic A-framed suspension bridge on 2nd Street completed in 1999. Mill Race Park by Michael Van Valkenburgh, along with structures by Stanley Saitowitz, were dedicated in 1992 and anchored the west end of 5th Street. The Visitors Center was expanded in 1995 with an addition by Kevin Roche. The city retained an executive architect, William Johnson to continue to implement many of Kennon's concepts. Robert A. M. Stern and Associates provided another downtown plan in 2002. A new Central Middle School designed by Ralph Johnson of Perkins+Will was completed in 2007 on 5th Street.

In 2005, a second Columbus Redevelopment Commission had to again focus on radical downtown redevelopment due to the failing retail mall and the substantial costs projected to maintain the original Commons. They began with an economic strategic plan. Koetter Kim & Associates was hired, recommended by Cesar Pelli, to create a master plan for the creation of a downtown "entertainment district", with a emphasis on the reuse of The Commons structure, the need for more downtown parking, and the establishment of mixed uses including work, education, housing and street front retail. While this master plan was implemented though the "Great Recession" which began in December 2007, it has realized many major projects including three downtown parking garages, the reestablishment of Jackson Street with new retail facades, a hotel, the new Commons, a general office building for Cummins and its expansion, new apartments and many new downtown restaurants with sidewalk dining.

Miller House and Garden *(photo courtesy of Indianapolis Museum of Art)*

National Recognition of Columbus, Indiana

Columbus, Indiana is nationally and internationally recognized for its modern architecture and landscape architecture. It has been referred to as "a veritable museum of modern architecture," "a small-town architectural mecca" and "the Athens of the prairie."

The buildings and the architects who designed buildings in Columbus have been recognized for design excellence by some of the most prestigious architectural awards:

7 National Historic Landmarks
Designated by the National Park Service, United States Department of the Interior for historic landmarks that "possess exceptional value and quality in illustrating or interpreting the heritage of the United States."
See page 198 for nomination summary.
- First Christian Church, Eliel Saarinen
- Irwin Union Bank, Eero Saarinen, Dan Kiley
- Miller House, Eero Saarinen, Dan Kiley, Alexander Girard
- Mabel McDowell School, John Carl Warnecke
- North Christian Church, Eero Saarinen, Dan Kiley
- First Baptist Church, Harry Weese, Dan Kiley
- The Republic, Myron Goldsmith (SOM)

5 American Institute of Architects (AIA) Architecture Honor Award buildings
The highest national honor for a building
- Lincoln Elementary School, Gunnar Birkerts
- The Republic, Myron Goldsmith (SOM)
- Columbus East H.S., Mitchell-Giurgola
- Cummins Health Center, Hardy Holzman Pfeiffer Associates
- AT&T Switching Center, Paul Kennon (CRS)

8 AIA Gold Medal winners
The highest national honor for an architect
- Eliel Saarinen
- Eero Saarinen
- Kevin Roche
- Romaldo Giurgola
- Richard Meier
- I.M. Pei
- Edward Larrabee Barnes
- Cesar Pelli

4 Pritzker Architecture Prize winners
The highest international honor for an architect
- Kevin Roche
- I.M. Pei
- Richard Meier
- Robert Venturi

Over the years, the perception of the success and the value of modern architecture for the community has been mixed. The following are excepts from national journals:

Columbus, IN...A Study in Small-Town Progress
Architectural Forum, October 1955:
"Few towns of its size enjoy as much good new architecture, both downtown and in the suburbs. The big church and the little bank have set the pace for future improvements downtown. But as Columbus continues to refurbish and rebuild, it will continue to need good professional advice. To keep its character and continuity, it must preserve not only the high standard of its best new buildings, but the rich history of its best old ones."

Athens of the Prairie
Saturday Evening Post, March 21, 1964:
"As a motorist rolls toward Columbus, Ind., he will see little that distinguishes it from other Midwestern towns. The countryside… yields to the usual commercial blight. …a nondescript shopping center, …Then, predictably, there are the old Victorian homes and the humdrum ranch-style houses. But suddenly there is the unexpected: one building, then another, that seems to have been plucked out of a city of the future.

"The townspeople view all this architectural splendor with a mixture of pride, bewilderment, annoyance and amusement. The roof of a modernistic bank by Eero Saarinen is topped with inverted cups that look like halved tennis balls. One Hoosier has labeled it 'The Brassiere Factory.' Harry Weese's red-brick Northside Junior High School, with its old arched factory windows and rectangular boxlike shape, is fondly called 'the Penitentiary.' And a Weese-designed bank with air conditioning towers rising stiffly from all four corners is known simply as the 'Dead Horse.'

"As a whole, Columbus will never be a delight to the eye. But one way people learn the difference between the mediocre and the imaginative is to live with both. Today the citizens of Columbus are in a better position than most Americans to make that distinction."

Symphony in Stone, *1967:*
When First Lady, Mrs. Lyndon "Ladybird" Johnson visited Columbus in 1967, she noted "It is said that architecture is 'Frozen Music' but seldom in history has such a group of devoted artists produced such a **'Symphony in Stone'** as presents itself to the eye in Columbus, Indiana".

Columbus, Indiana:
The Town that Architecture Made Famous
Architectural Forum, December 1965:

"Columbus does have a few good buildings that Miller is not connected with in some way. In 1959 the Hamilton Foundation (another local philanthropy concerned about design) gave the town an ice rink with a playful clubhouse by Weese. The First Baptist Church, also by Weese, is the most striking evidence to date that Miller's enthusiasm is rubbing off on others.

"The transformation of downtown Columbus is not awaiting the making of large plans. A small but significant civic plaza will be created as part of the design for a new county library by I. M. Pei & Associates.

"The most encouraging sign for the future of Columbus is the recent recognition by civic leaders that isolated masterpieces may make the town famous, but never great. There is reason to hope that visitors to Columbus in 1975 will find it a showplace of urban design as well as architecture."

Columbus, Indiana, Grows Used to Its Fine Architecture.
George Vecsey, New York Times, May 17, 1971:

"On your left, ladies and gentlemen, the striking green sign of Early Holiday Inn Period. And on your right, the fabled orange roof sometimes known as Classic Howard Johnson.

"This is the only view of Columbus, Ind., from the highway – just another town between Seymour and Franklin on Interstate 65, heralded by the orange roof and green sign of modern neon and plastic America.

"But this afternoon, …they held a dedication for a library designed by I. M. Pei of New York and a sculpture by Henry Moore of England. And these works are not exactly slumming in Columbus.

"Because Columbus is on the flat lands, the Saturday Evening Post called it "the Athens of the prairie," with some sarcasm, a decade ago. Everybody knows what happened to the Saturday Evening Post. Meanwhile, Columbus proudly uses the slogan on its welcome billboards and today the townspeople applauded the work of I. M. Pei and Henry Moore.

"None of this was visible from the cars that whizzed by on the cement interstate – but the residents of Columbus know what they have."

Prairie Showplace
Paul Goldberger, New York Times, April 4, 1976:

"It is a strange town, because it is still very much a settlement on the prairie – the stores are full on Saturday morning, the churches are full on Sunday morning and nothing much is full late at night. Washington Street is the main commercial street, and it is a model of the old-fashioned Main Street, as if out of Disneyland. But in and among the well-crafted Victorian storefront buildings that could be anywhere are buildings that exist only in Columbus…

"The overall environment is an odd combination of small-town ordinariness and big-city slickness. "There is another faction in town that had disapproved of the whole business from the start. There are occasional letters to The Republic denouncing Irwin Miller and suggesting that the high-design architects he has brought to town go against the Midwestern grain of simplicity, and there are others that argue that quality design has cost too much, even with Cummins picking up the architect's fees.

"There is great power in a great individual building. But often a group of buildings, even a group as distinguished as that which had made Columbus famous, fails to come together to create a coherent whole.

"A shift to broader questions of urban design, if indeed it is taking place in Columbus, does not invalidate the importance of the single buildings.

"But broader concerns make it possible for Columbus to begin to look at itself in a fuller, more complex way, to come to grips with the problems of what architecture can and cannot do. Columbus's remarkable buildings do not offer any easy answers, but they pose all the right questions."

A Most Uncommon Town: Columbus, Indiana
National Geographic. September 1978:

"For townspeople the forty-plus buildings designed by modern masters of architecture do not make a spectator sport. They are places to learn in, pray in, read in, have fun in, work in, bank in, have daily life of the community written and printed in. Small town in scale, they fit in like slightly eccentric neighbors, adding variety, provoking debate, and stimulating a taste for the unconventional."

Architecture: Hoosier Mecca for Modern Architecture
Ellen Posner, Wall Street Journal, Jan. 16, 1984:

"What is missing in Columbus…are those visual sequences – of buildings, trees, streets and open land – both accidental and planned, that work together to create a fabric and, by doing so, a strong sense of place.

"It would not be unreasonable to expect that a city that is famous for its architecture to have this sort of fabric. Many less famous cities certainly do. In downtown Columbus, … everything is scattered, isolated, mismatched.

"On Washington Street, a less-than-bustling commercial street where many of the stores are empty, a huge, enclosed shopping mall designed by Cesar Pelli turns a blank brown-glass face to its environment.

"Some attention has been paid to this problem. Skidmore Owings created a master plan for downtown Columbus in the late 1960s… The architects have just updated the master plan, which now addresses the issues of "streetscape," "townscape," "point of entry," restoration of historic buildings, and the need for a suitable hotel. Not a moment too soon. Enormous amounts of time, energy, and talent have been spent on the built environment in Columbus, and residents of that town deserve to have the result be something greater, not less than, the sum of its parts."

The Making of a Model City:
J. Irwin Miller and his Vision for Columbus, Ind.
Benjamin Forgey, Washington Post. Oct. 8, 1986:

"Miller, 77, will fly to Washington today on a Cummins company plane to become the first living American to be inducted into a new pantheon, The Building Hall of Fame, established by the National Building Museum... Even more telling of esteem for Miller is the Who's Who list of living architects happily accepting the invitations to pay homage.

"Architecture," he says, "is something you can see. You can't see a spirit or a temperament or a character, though, and there's an invisible part of this community that I'm very proud of… My interest is much more in trying to be a responsible citizen… It (the Cummins architecture program) preserves the democratic process in the best sense, and in a democracy I think that the process is more important than the product."

Goodbye, Columbus
Philip Nobel, Metropolis, June 19, 2006:

"J. Irwin Miller thought that architecture could save the world – or at least his small corner of it: Columbus, Indiana… The place only lacks a Paul Rudolph and a Philip Johnson to make it a truly encyclopedic collection from the period in which architects were shedding the formal dogmas of Modern architecture but not yet its social code: the belief that good buildings, property deployed, could make new cities great and reform dying ones – architecture could save the world.

"The utopianism at the heart of the Modern movement was hard to shake.

"Miller drank that Kool-Aid.

"The downtown is, for all intents and purposes, dead. Even a restaurant there that once made a guide of Indiana's best has joined the row of shuttered businesses. This fate was hastened by the construction in 1973 of a bronze-glass downtown mall…years before the Wal-Mart built out by the intersection of Taylor Road and route 31. Cruising those thoroughfares, predictably, one finds the rest of the town as it is actually lived in…all the interchangeable parts of our interchangeable sprawl.

"Would Columbus not be a better place today had all that energy and funding gone into, say, a concerted program of creative urban planning – the best minds focused on the creation of the best space, achieved through the invisible, unsexy means of zoning and finance and codes? The town might not look as cool – it would be deprived of the income that architourism brings, but it might be a safer and happier place to live."

Mid-Century Time Capsule
Allen G. Brake, The Architect's Newspaper (online), May 25, 2011:

"Columbus, Indiana is known for its quotidian modernism, where schools, firehouses, churches, and parks are well designed and also accessible. The luxurious modernism of the Miller House was a private reserve where every detail was considered but only the family and their guests could experience it. Now open to all, it is a fascinating counterpoint to the everyday modernism that defines the town. The last of the Miller children has decamped for a job in New York, and the house has the slightly forlorn look so common to house museums. But the architecture program the family started is alive and well. Three new buildings… will be completed or break ground this year. The patrons may be gone, but the town remains their true legacy."

J. Irwin Miller

Eero Saarinen

Harry Weese

Gunnar Birkerts

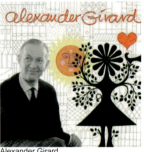
Alexander Girard

Dan Kiley

Kevin Roche

Cesar Pelli

Paul Kennon

I. M. Pei

Robert Venturi

Paul Kevin Kennon

Thomas Beeby

Robert A.M. Stern

Debra Berke

Will Miller

Fred Koetter

Carlos Jimenez

The Commons is an example of collaboration and connections. The connections begin with the initial recommendation of Cesar Pelli by Kevin Roche to design The Commons Mall project. Both had worked together at Eero Saarinen's office. Cesar Pelli recommended Jean Tinguely to create an interactive sculpture within the unique indoor public space that he created. Pelli would later recommend Fred Koetter and Susie Kim to do the downtown master plan involving the revitalization of the original Commons and Commons Mall, whose redesign Koetter Kim & Associates ultimately led with CSO Architects. Cesar Pelli and Fred Koetter had both been chairs of the School of Architecture at Yale University, and I was a student of Fred Koetter at the Harvard University Graduate School of Design. The Commons design team recommended Tom Luckey, an architect and artist educated at Yale University, to design the interactive playground sculpture. The ultimate design collaboration on The Commons project was the extensive public and private foundation involvement, not only in fund raising, but also in "client" design committee involvement, that resulted in a new and improved building that everyone contributed to and collaborated with to create a distinctive design, with reminiscence of the original design.

This edition has attempted to identify the design collaborations within the modern architecture section and the architect's connections within the appendix. I am fortunate to have been involved in many projects in Columbus as the lead designer or a collaborating designer. I cease to be amazed by the unique collaborations and connections that make Columbus, Indiana different by design.

Steven R. Risting, architect

Connections, Collaboration, Community

The realization of the nationally recognized architecture and art in Columbus, Indiana is the result of collaboration and connections. It began with the collaboration of the public and private - an offer from J. Irwin Miller from Cummins Engine, Inc. to the public school board that evolved into The Cummins Foundation Architecture Program. It expanded to local church and business leaders hiring nationally prominent architects. And it includes architects recommending internationally prominent artist to design art or sculpture that are an integral part of the architectural experience.

The connections to the selection of these architects and artists can be initially credited to J. Irwin Miller and the Irwin, Sweeney and Miller families, and to the recommendations of the architects themselves. The connections to the selection of prominent architects is further noted in the discovery of collaborating designers within the architect's office such as Eero Saarinen and Harry Weese, or the schools of architecture at Cranbrook Academy, Yale University, and Harvard University. Eero Saarinen's connections were especially significant with his friendship to Harry Weese from Cranbrook to the numerous prominent architects that worked in his office as collaborating designers, draftsman or model builders, including Kevin Roche, John Dinkeloo, Gunnar Birkerts, Robert Venturi, Cesar Pelli, Bruce Adams, Paul Kennon, and Balthazar Korab, as well as the design collaborations with Dan Kiley and Alexander Girard.

The Yale University connection is especially strong. While J. Irwin Miller and Eero Saarinen both attended Yale University, they did not meet there. Many of the Columbus architects have been associated with the Yale University School of Design, including Cesar Pelli, Thomas Beeby, Fred Koetter and Robert A.M. Stern as chairs, and Bruce Adams and Deborah Berke as professors. There was a brief connection to Harvard University with the selection of John Johansen and Eliot Noyes of the "Harvard Five", as well as several of the architects educated at the Harvard University Graduate School of Design.

While the focus is typically on crediting the architectural design to a lead architect, it is also important to recognize the collaborating designer within the architectural firms, whether firm partners or associates. This has become especially evident in the recognition of the significant design leadership of Kevin Roche with the Miller House, and the design leadership of Ben Weese for Northside Middle School and the Hope bank. The collaborative design partnerships are recognized with such examples as Eero Saarinen with Eliel Saarinen of Eliel and Eero Saarinen Architects at First Christian Church: John Dinkeloo with Kevin Roche of Kevin Roche John Dinkeloo and Associates at the Columbus Post Office; Jack Hartray with Harry Weese at First Baptist Church; Michael Ross with Hugh Hardy, Malcolm Holzman, Norman Pfeiffer of Hardy Holzman Pfeiffer Associates at Cummins Occupational Health Association; Truitt Garrison with Paul Kennon of Caudill Rowlett Scott at AT&T Switching Center; and Gary Ainge with Thomas Beeby of Hammond Beeby and Babka at Breeden Realtors Office Building. In the last decade, the association and collaboration of national architects with local architects have become more of the norm; this has included Jim Paris, Nolan Bingham, Todd Williams, Ratio Architects and CSO Architects, who have also completed significant designs on their own that have contributed to the architectural context of Columbus.

The role of the client cannot be underestimated in the collaborative design process. J. Irwin Miller noted that "Great architecture is... a triple achievement. It is the solving of a concrete problem. It is the free expression of the architect himself. And it is an inspired and intuitive expression of the client." While the client's role is obvious in typically establishing the project ("the problem") and the site, he also accepts and rejects the design, and is active but not too dominant in the design process. While many of the buildings in Columbus are modest in scale, compared to many of the projects that made the national architect famous, they still have the architect's indelible design signature.

"We shape our buildings, and afterwards our buildings shape us."
       Winston Churchill, 1943

"It is expensive to be mediocre in this world. Quality has always been cost effective. The tragic mistake in history that's always been made by the well-to-do is that they have feathered their own nests. Today we know that society does not survive unless it works for everybody."
       J. Irwin Miller, 1987

"Everyone of us lives and moves all his life within the limitations, sight and influence of architecture - at home, at school, at church, at work. The influence of architecture with which we are surrounded in our youth affects our lives, our standards, our tastes when we are grown, just as the influence of the parents and teachers with which we are surrounded in out youth affects us as adults.

American architecture has never had more creative, imaginative practitioners than it has today. Each of the best of today's architects can contribute something of lasting value to Columbus."
       J. Irwin Miller, 2001

A Look at Modern Architecture in Columbus, Indiana

This section documents a majority of the major modern buildings and parks in Columbus, Indiana, designed predominantly by nationally and internationally recognized architects, landscape architects and interior designers from 1942 to 2012. Each project has been recently photographed in its current condition, including when appropriate interior spaces and architectural details. A building plan and architect's sketch are included, if available.

The date of the project is its completion date. If known, the date the project was commissioned is noted, typically shown as a range of 2 to 5 years including the time from the initial design through completion. The project name is its current name, with its original name listed if changed. Each project is typically associated with a lead design architect, which is also supplemented with the name and location of the architectural firm the designer was associated with and any key associates or collaborating designers working with the lead architect. In the last decade it has become more common for national architects to associate with local architects, who are also listed. The project narrative is concise to give a brief description of the building or landscape.

The architect's design statement or the client's design intention is included, if available. Projects with the design architect's fee paid for by the Cummins Foundation Architecture Program, as well as projects completed by Cummins, are identified with the Cummins logo.

A chronological and alphabetical list of the modern buildings, and an alphabetical list of the architects is included in the Appendix.

Several of the projects also have major public art work associated with it, typically recommended by the design architect. These are noted, but included in the Public Art section.

The historic buildings of Columbus, with their preservation, restoration, or rehabilitation with additions, are as important to the architectural character of this community as is the modern design. Selected historic buildings are included in the last section.

1942 First Christian Church

1939 - 1942   531 Fifth Street   *originally called* Tabernacle Christ Church

Eliel Saarinen
Eliel and Eero Saarinen, Architects
Bloomfield Hills, Michigan

Collaborating designers
Loja Saarinen
Eero Saarinen
Charles Eames

2002
Addition
& Renovation

Nolan Bingham
Paris-Bingham Partnership
Columbus, Indiana

Client's statement:
"There is no traditional architectural style that could be successfully employed to express our purpose. For generations the basic pattern of church structure has remained practically unchanged. At best the recent designs have been recreations of traditional styles. None of these could fully express the grandeur and yet simplicity of Christian faith unencumbered by human creeds and human symbolism. The only alternative was to find an architect whose creative genius would make possible the realization of such an expressive building. This was accomplished when Eliel Saarinen consented to accept this commission."
Rev. T.K. Smith, 1943

The First Christian Church was the first contemporary building in Columbus and one of the first churches of contemporary architecture in the United States. The geometric simplicity of the building's design is seen in the rectangular box that houses the sanctuary and the 166-foot high campanile (bell tower) that has become the iconic symbol of Columbus' modern architecture.

The building actually occupies an entire city block, with a two-story classroom wing supported on columns and piers, and a sunken garden originally containing a reflecting pool which provided a civic place. The building's exterior is primarily a buff brick with limestone accents, the main entry facade is a 10 x 12 grid with a slightly offset entry and a stone cross. The facade stonework, including columns, benches, and exterior baptistry fonts feature relief detailing typical at the Cranbrook Academy.

The slightly offset symmetry of the exterior reveals itself with the asymmetrical and functional interiors. Eliel Saarinen noted that "We have not been concerned with a symmetrical solution... the function of the chancel, is asymmetrical in its nature." The sanctuary features an offset cross above a wood screen wall that opens up to reveal the baptistry behind, a skewed side wood screen wall with a pipe organ behind, and an offset piano shaped pulpit. The tall sanctuary space has high vertical windows on the west and a one-story entry corridor on the east. The wood pews were custom designed by Charles Eames. The tapestry on the front east wall, "The Sermon on the Mount", was designed by Eliel and his wife, Loja. There is also a small chapel with similar functional asymmetry and wood screens.

In 2002, a two-story classroom was added to the south side, distinguished from the original building with a slightly contrasting brick.

National Historic Landmark, 2000

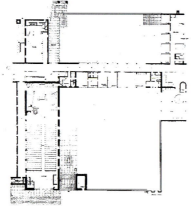

Original Floor Plan

1954 Irwin Union Bank

1950 - 1954   500 Washington Street

Eero Saarinen
Eero Saarinen and Associates
Bloomfield Hills, Michigan

Landscape Architect
Dan Kiley
Charlotte, Vermont

Architect's comments (letter to a friend):
*"It is going to be a bank without any pompousness, absolutely no intention to impress. All it is is a very low glass enclosed marketplace-like little building in the middle of town...
It also has nine cupolas, just like San Marco. All this sounds a bit bad but it really isn't."*
Eero Saarinen, June 1952

The one-story glass pavilion was one of the first open plan and transparent banks in the United States. It was a dramatic contrast to the typical classical stone or brick banks located across the street. The square plan is setback from the main street, and is surrounded by trees and planting beds, creating a "pavilion in the park". The trees on Washington Street maintain the scale of the Victorian facades.

The open plan and transparency created a friendly environment for banking. The teller's counters were also open, not behind "cages", to allow for a more personal interaction between the customer and the banker. A couple of offices and a meeting room are located within the interior volume, like a piece of custom wood furniture. The open office desks were custom designed by Eero Saarinen and produced by furniture maker Herman Miller. The 11'-6" high ceiling features nine opaque domes, not skylights, which act as giant lamp shades reflecting the central custom light fixture. The perimeter 4'-6" overhang provides shading for the glass walls. The domes on the roof have motivated some observers to dub the bank "the brassiere factory."

The building is actually three components: the glass pavilion, a basement with the bank vault and meeting rooms, and an adjacent blank-walled office building with two glass connectors. The basement is accessed by an exquisite floating staircase suspended by steel rods in the middle of the plan. The bank also had one of the first drive-up teller windows, that was later expanded with additional remote drive-up lanes.

The building no longer functions as a bank. Cummins has purchased the building and is committed to preserving its historic value.

National Historic Landmark, 2000

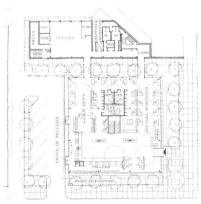

Original Plan

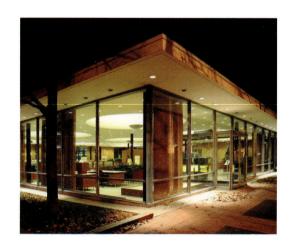

1957 Miller House & Garden
1953 - 1957

Eero Saarinen
Eero Saarinen and Associates
Bloomfield Hills, Michigan

Collaborating designers
Kevin Roche
Balthazar Korab

Interior Design
Alexander Girard
Sante Fe, New Mexico

Landscape Architect
Dan Kiley
Charlotte, Vermont

"America's Most Significant Modernist House"
Travel + Leisure magazine, 2010

"Miller House and Garden, as many have noted, is a remarkable place - a remarkable modernist masterpiece that is unexpected in a south-central Indiana city, ...remarkable for the will and commitment of J. Irwin Miller and Xenia Simons Miller, who commissioned and cared for it; and remarkable for the perfection of its design by three of twentieth-century America's leading talents: Eero Saarinen, Alexander Girard, and Dan Kiley."
    Bradley Brooks
    Indianapolis Museum of Art

J. Irwin Miller and Xenia Simons Miller commissioned Eero Saarinen and Alexander Girard in 1953 to design a residence for their family, one that could also serve as a showcase for entertaining corporate clients and dignitaries. The house expands upon the international Modernist architectural aesthetics with an open and flowing layout, flat roof and stone and glass walls. The floor plan is configured with four enclosed private zones "pin wheeling" around the central open living and entertaining space, all configured beneath a grid of skylights supported by cruciform steel columns. The central living space features a sunken conversational pit. The interiors are filled with textiles and decorative objects that feature strong colors and playful patterns that enliven the finely textured marble walls and travertine floors.

Amid the residence's large geometric gardens, its grandest feature is an allée of honey locust trees that runs along the west side of the house. In 2000, the Miller House and Garden became the first National Historic Landmark to receive its designation while one of its designers, landscape architect Dan Kiley, was still living and while still occupied by its original owners.

The Miller House and Garden is one of the finest expressions of American modernism, an integration of house and landscape that draws upon historical precedents without repeating them, enfolding them in a compelling composition of forms and spaces that captures the genius of its designers, the aspirations of its owners, and the spirit of their time. The property is owned and cared for by the Indianapolis Museum of Art. Tours at Miller House and Garden are available through the Columbus Area Visitors Center.

National Historic Landmark, 2000

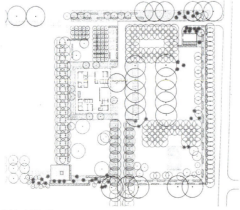

Original Site Plan

photo courtesy of Indianapolis Museum of Art

photos this page courtesy of Indianapolis Museum of Art

photos this page courtesy of Indianapolis Museum of Art

1957 Lillian C. Schmitt Elementary School

1955 - 1957   1057 27th Street

Harry Weese
Harry Weese and Associates
Chicago, Illinois

Collaborating designer
Brewster (Bruce) Adams

1991 Addition   **Andrea Leers, Jane Weinzapfel**
Leers, Weinzapfel & Associates
Boston, Massachusetts

The original Lillian C. Schmitt Elementary School, included a kindergarten and twelve classrooms, designed with a natural blend of brick, glass and wood. The school, named for Miss Lillian Schmitt (1891-1959), a elementary teacher for 43 years, was the first in a series of new schools named in honor of local educators.

Each classroom has a shallow peaked roof line, making an interesting zigzag exterior silhouette. The ten classrooms have large windows opening directly onto planned playground areas. Small skylights and wood planking highlight the low ceilings of the corridors, providing warmth and scale. In the center of the building, the original large, hexagonal multi-purpose room with a high ceiling could be enlarged by opening folding doors into the main corridor or into the cafeteria. This room has been transformed into a multi-media and computer center at the heart of the school. A new entry is in the forecourt formed by the original and new corridor wings.

The addition consists of two parts: the first extends the existing classroom corridor into a new two-story classroom group; the second creates a new parallel corridor and gallery containing all special spaces (kindergartens, art, music, science, gymnasium and cafeteria). While the red painted steel frame with concrete block infill contrast, the proportions and scale of the window patterns compliment the original design.

The Cummins Foundation made its first grant to support architects fees for this school, with the desire to provide an alternative to the standard, but uninspiring, school buildings being built in baby boom era of the late 1950s and early 1960s. That design grant, repeated several times for other public facilities, eventually became the Cummins Foundation Architecture Program.

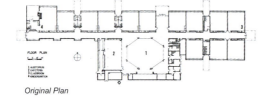
Original Plan

Original & Addition architect's fees paid by
The Cummins Foundation
Architecture Program

Rendering of original design

1958 Hamilton Center Ice Arena

2501 25th Street *originally called* Lincoln Center community building and ice rink

Harry Weese
Harry Weese and Associates
Chicago, Illinois

Collaborating designer
Brewster (Bruce) Adams

1975 Addition

Koster & Associates
Cleveland, Ohio

Architect's comments:
"The design is a kind of Black Forest stage setting for exhilarating evenings under the stars. But the daytime must also be considered - hence, the permanent natural materials, the opaqueness and the symmetry, all conspiring toward a civic, if informal, character."
Harry Weese

The original Swiss chalet style building was designed by Harry Weese as a community building with warming house and changing rooms for an outdoor refrigerated ice rink. The facility was a gift to the Columbus community by the Hamilton Foundation to provide winter recreational activities. Harry Weese was selected as the architect because of his imagination and his philosophy of creating architectural beauty while fulfilling needs at the same time.

The building exterior features rough-hewn granite boulder battered walls and glass with views to the exterior. The interior features triple-peaked roof with wood beams and planking. A central granite fireplace, highlighting the spacious interior, is surrounded by wooden benches, an inviting sight to chilled skaters. The floor material is skate-resistant.

Because of an increased community interest in ice skating and the need to extend the skating season, the community decided to enclose the outdoor rink in 1975. Koster and Associates designed the enclosure of the large ice arena as an extension of the existing center with similar exterior materials and architectural details. Enlarged to a regulation-sized hockey rink and an adjacent practice rink, the facility now offers year-round skating.

Hamilton Center Ice Arena, the adjacent lighted tennis courts, softball diamonds, handball courts, playgrounds and multi-purpose recreation area of Lincoln Park are maintained by the Columbus Parks and Recreation department.

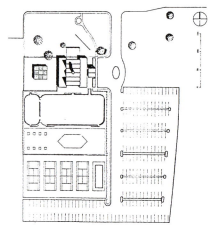
Original site plan with exterior ice rink

Architect's fees supported by
The Hamilton Foundation
as a memorial to B.F. Hamilton, COSCO founder.

Original exterior ice rink (photo courtesty of Columbus Indiana Archtitectural Archives)

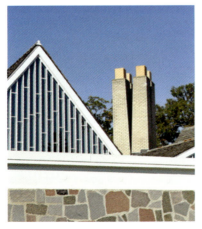

1958 Hope Branch Bank

645 Harrison Street, Hope, Indiana

originally Irwin Union Bank

Harry Weese
Ben Weese, *project designer*
Harry Weese and Associates
Chicago, Illinois

This small branch bank is located on the west side of the downtown square in Hope, Indiana. It is a simple rectangular plan with twelve pyramidal roofs expressed on the exterior and the interior. The roof/ceiling "floats" above the exterior brick walls with a glass clerestory window on all sides. The roof is supported by small steel columns that are only three inches square at the top and bottom, larger in the middle.

The building entry is expressed with an additional pyramidal canopy at the front and a full glass window. The entry is an exquisitely detailed glass vestibule including a glass ceiling. The interior vault and enclosed offices are kept below the clerestory windows, allowing the entire interior volume of the building with its multiple peaked ceiling to be experienced when in the main banking space. The teller counter and check writing table are original designs.

The exterior rust red brick is simply detailed with soldier course sills at the clerestory windows and recessed corners that feature round downspouts which appear to support the floating roof.

1960 Mabel McDowell Adult Education Center

2700 McKinley Avenue

originally Mabel McDowell Elementary School

John Carl Warnecke
John Carl Warnecke & Associates
San Francisco, California

1983 Remodeling	Conversion to Adult Education Center
2012 Renovations	CSO Architects Indianapolis, Indiana

Architect's statement:
"A dominant characteristic of Southern Indiana is the flat terrain, a horizontal theme accentuated by tall Victorian houses, barns and silos, with picturesque groves of trees. The school design is based on the creation of a similar grouping of masses and spaces into a scheme which focuses the school group into its own controlled environment, yet extends it outward into the community."
John Carl Warnecke

Mabel McDowell Adult Education Center was originally designed as an elementary school with four clusters of pavilion-type classroom buildings surrounding a central grouping of support buildings, with landscaped courtyards in between and in the center. McDowell was the first school built under the "park school" concept, with adjacent land and the building utilized year-round as a neighborhood playground.

The center buildings contain administrative offices, a multi-purpose auditorium/gymnasium, a cafeteria/kitchen, kindergarten, a special-ed classroom, music and art rooms. The multipurpose room is topped with a pyramidal skylight. The four corner buildings, each containing three classrooms, a storage room and restrooms are connected to the nucleus buildings by covered walkways and patio areas. Wooden trellises create deep eaves to shade the large expanses of windows in the steel-framed buildings.

Originally designed to serve elementary students, the school's design flexibility was demonstrated by the 1983 conversion to an adult education facility. The adult education center offers a variety of classes including basic literacy and English as a second language. The 2012 renovation included window and metal panel replacement, and a day care located in the original kindergarten classrooms.

This school is named in honor of Miss Mabel McDowell (1880-1961), an elementary school teacher in Columbus for 25 years.

National Historic Landmark, 2000

Architect's fees paid by
The Cummins Foundation
Architecture Program

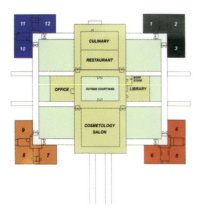

Adult Education Center Plan

34

1961 Northside Middle School

2700 Maple Street

Harry Weese
Ben Weese, *project designer*
Harry Weese and Associates
Chicago, Illinois

1991 Addition

Andrea Leers, Jane Weinzapfel
Leers, Weinzapfel & Associates
Boston, Massachusetts

Architect's statement:
"A firm statement of the dignity and prominence in the community that a school should possess."
Harry Weese

The distinguishing feature of this massive building is its repetitive use of brick arches, most of them inset with windows. A landscaped interior courtyard has been offset from the center of the building. The gymnasium/multipurpose room, often used for community events, and originally a regulation-size swimming pool were placed side by side, with entry from either the courtyard corridor or street side entrances. The hallways are also brick arches inset with lockers and clerestory windows above allowing natural light to filter into the halls from the classrooms. The brick bearing wall was selected as the most economical construction at the time. Harry Weese choose a three story building instead of the typical one level school because kids love to climb up and down stairs. Ben Weese, Harry's brother, was the primary building designer.

The one story addition continues the perimeter of the original building in both plan and elevation. Specialized areas for active learning, recreation and assembly in the new block are counterpoised to the quiet, traditional classroom spaces of the original building. The regular simple enclosure of the addition is punctuated by geometric volumes which push through the frame – a pyramid over the commons, industrial skylights over the art studios and a double-barrel vault over the cafeteria.

The relocated main entry leading to the commons marks the school's new center with a tall entry porch and a long south-facing portico. The simple circulation of the original school is extended into the addition to form an urban model of "streets" (corridors), "squares" (courtyard, commons), "public assembly rooms" (library, swimming pool, cafeteria, gymnasium) and "private dwellings" (classrooms and offices).

Original & Addition architect's fees paid by
The Cummins Foundation
Architecture Program

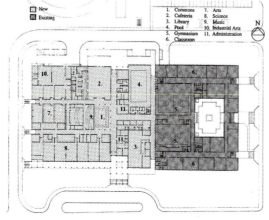

Plan with addition

1961 Eastbrook Plaza Branch Bank

25th Street and National Road   First Financial Bank (*originally* Irwin Union Bank)

Harry Weese
Ben Weese, *project manager*
Harry Weese and Associates
Chicago, Illinois

1996 Addition

Thomas Beeby
Gary M. Ainge
Hammond Beeby and Babka, Inc.
Chicago, Illinois

This branch bank was located adjacent to a newly opened shopping center and next to Haw Creek. The four brick towers, which originally housed drive-up windows and a depository, as well as mechanical units above, provide a prominent identity for the bank. The gray-glazed brick recalled the concrete of the adjacent bridge abutments. The architect said the crenelated towers and adjacent creek were reminiscent of a child's version of a castle. Locals have nicknamed the building the "dead horse".

The simple rectangular plan contains a one and a half story central space filled with natural light from the perimeter windows and clerestory windows between brick piers. The entry is a split-level with stairs stepping up to the main space and side stairs on both sides continuing up to the bank manager's office on the open mezzanine level. With the main hall raised above the parking lot, the views to the exterior are spectacular.

The 1996 addition was a modern drive-up banking canopy requiring fewer tellers. The canopy is supported by smaller brick towers, similar to the entry towers. ADA accessibility was also provided.

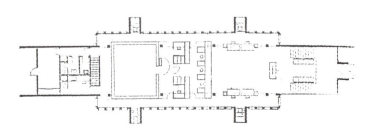

Original Floor Plan

1962 COSCO Inc. Office Building

2525 State Street

now Dorel Juvenile Group, Inc.

Harry Weese
Harry Weese and Associates
Chicago, Illinois

Landscape Architect
Dan Kiley
Charlotte, Vermont

The one-story brick office and research building was an addition to the existing manufacturing facility for COSCO (**CO**lumbus **S**pecialities **CO**mpany, now a part of Dorel Juvenile Group), which specialized in making card tables, chairs and baby car seats. Harry Weese was asked to redesign the industrial company facilities as well as to add a new research facility. The architect had previously designed the Lincoln Center community building and ice rink (now called the Hamilton Center Ice Arena) for the Hamilton Foundation to honor B.F. Hamiliton, the founder of COSCO, Inc.

The design is a simple modern brick building with a continuous "strip" window, typical of the many streamlined buildings of the time. The entry lobby is a projecting concrete box, with a meticulously detailed entry canopy and glass vestibule. The canopy columns are cruciform shaped that transition to beams on the flat plate concrete canopy.

The canopy is parallel to an allée of trees that define the edge and extend into the expansive parking lot. The landscape architect selected a variety of trees, including ginkgo, river birch, hornbeam and oak, as well as yews and a ground cover of euonymus. This provides a large open green space in an urban area.

Rendering

1962 Parkside Elementary School
1400 Parkside Drive

Norman Fletcher
The Architects Collaborative (TAC)
Cambridge, Massachusetts

1990 Addition
Norman Fletcher
The Architects Collaborative (TAC)
Cambridge, Massachusetts

"The Family" sculpture
Harris Barron, *sculptor*
Brookline Village, Massachusetts

2006 **Freedom Field Playground**

The identifying feature of Parkside Elementary School is the series of barrel vaults using wood beams, wood planking and steel columns, creating an umbrella effect. The same architectural device is repeated in the central multi-purpose section and the barrel vault roof of the new gymnasium addition which dominates the rear of the school.

The design of this school utilizes an educational approach emphasizing the individual within his or her own age group. The original building consisted of three buildings including two classroom wings and the central multipurpose area with cafeteria, auditorium and playroom, connected with courtyards. The building is raised on a two-foot podium of earth, with recessed courtyards and play areas, to provide a change of experience from the otherwise flat landscape. The brick classroom wings feature deep laminated wood beams that project beyond the exterior wall to provide shading to the large windows and clerestory windows below. The 1990 addition enclosed the courtyards with special education classrooms and kindergarten, as well as a large gymnasium. In the central courtyard stands "The Family" sculpture,

Sports and play areas are important elements of the site and form an uncluttered, yet active, background for the school. Freedom Field was specially designed to be entirely handicapped accessible, allowing the interaction of physically challenged and able-bodied children and parents. Two Columbus mothers were instrumental in the idea to create a playground that could be used by children with disabilities. The sports field and playground are operated by the Columbus Parks and Recreation department.

Original & Addition architect's fees paid by
The Cummins Foundation
Architecture Program

1963 Administrative Building

2650 Home Avenue *now* BCSC Information Services building

Norman Fletcher
The Architects Collaborative (TAC)
Cambridge, Massachusetts

This two-story octagonal brick building originally served as the headquarters for the administrative offices of the Bartholomew Consolidated School Corporation (BCSC). It is located next to Schmitt Elementary School, and in the vicinity of Northside Middle School and North High School. The building now houses BCSC's Information Services.

The building corners are highlighted with vertical brick piers with full height windows on each side. Each side features a blank brick wall in the center. The entry is highlighted with expansive glass windows, with vertical concrete fins on the second floor and large glass windows below with a solid door in the center. Low brick walls extend out into the landscape to create an entry courtyard.

The lobby features a curved staircase with cantilevered concrete treads that extend out of the curved brick wall rising in the center of the building. The roof peaks above the stairwell with an eight-panel glass dome which allows natural light to highlight the interior. Offices fan out and surround this center.

The Board of Trustees of the Bartholomew Consolidated School Corporation was recognized by the Indiana Arts Commission in 1973 for accepting the challenge of the community to build better schools.

Architect's fees paid by
The Cummins Foundation
Architecture Program

1964 North Christian Church
1959 - 1964   850 Tipton Lane

Eero Saarinen
Eero Saarinen and Associates
Bloomfield Hills, Michigan

Collaborating designers
Kevin Roche, John Dinkeloo
Alexander Girard, Paul Kennon, John Kinsella

Landscape Architect
Dan Kiley
Charlotte, Vermont

Architect's letters to J. Irwin Miller:
"We have finally to solve this church so that it can become a great building. I feel I have this obligation to the congregation, and as an architect, I have that obligation to my profession and my ideals. I want to solve it so that as an architect when I face St. Peter I am able to say that out of the buildings I did during my lifetime, one of the best was this little church, because it has in it a real spirit that speaks forth to all Christians as a witness to their faith."
    Eero Saarinen, April 1961

"I think we have finally solved the Columbus church."
    Eero Saarinen, July 1961

Eero Saarinen worked closely with members of the congregation to understand the church's theology, traditions and expectations, as well as its leadership in the growing concept of an ecumenical faith.

The sloping roof of this six sided building blends with the landscaped earth mound which surrounds it. This low line accentuates the slender 192 foot spire, topped with a five and a half foot tall gold leaf cross, which gives the church its distinctive design. Direct natural light enters the sanctuary through an oculus high in the ceiling at the base of the spire, and other natural lighting is diffused from under the edge of the roof line. The west building entry is a drop-off with a small chapel inside. The metal baptistry cover was designed by Alexander Girard. The east entry is the main entry directly into the sanctuary from the beautifully landscaped parking lot bounded by topiary hedges. The church sits in a parklike setting with natural landscaping, as well as a groove of magnolia trees and Dan Kiley's signature allée of trees.

The church is symmetrically designed to make the sanctuary the center of the church and the communion table the center of the sanctuary, so that the worship service is the focal point. On a tiered platform, twelve pedestal tables symbolic of the twelve disciples, are assembled as the communion table. At one end is a higher pedestal – the Christ table, which holds a silver chalice and a loaf of bread, the elements for communion. Opposite the main entrance are the pulpit, choir loft and a Holtkamp organ, the last organ designed by Walter Holtkamp, Sr.

This is the last building designed by Eero Saarinen before his untimely death on September 1, 1961. Roche Dinkeloo & Associates, the successor architectural firm, completed the building.

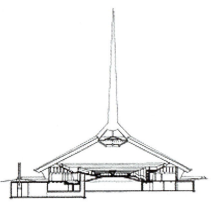

National Historic Landmark, 2000

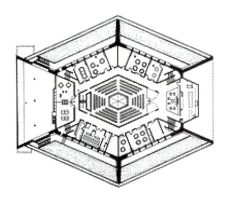

Floor Plan

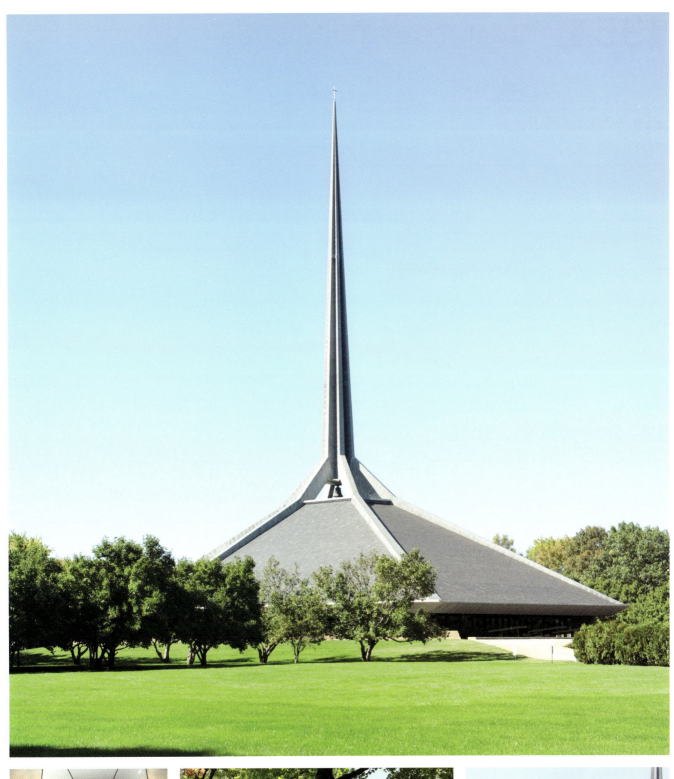
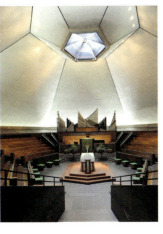

1964 Otter Creek Clubhouse

11522 East 50 North

Harry Weese
Harry Weese and Associates
Chicago, Illinois

Landscape Architect
Dan Kiley
Charlotte, Vermont

Golf Course
Robert Trent Jones
Montclair, New Jersey

1995 Golf Course Expansion

Rees Jones
Greg Muirhead, *co-designer*
Montclair, New Jersey

2010 Scoreboard

Kevin Roche
Hamden, Connecticut

Clubhouse & Golf Course
Architect's fees paid by
The Cummins Foundation
Architecture Program

As one approaches Otter Creek Clubhouse and Golf Course, located five miles east of Columbus, the first impression is of the compatibility of the building and its setting. The rural feeling of these modern building is achieved through the extensive use of wood. The precision of the building's geometric patterns compliment the orderliness of the 27-hole golf course.

The Clubhouse includes spacious lounge and dining areas that overlook the golf course. The floor to ceiling perimeter windows are protected by thin shed roofs that create surrounding porches. The golf course landscape extensively uses native trees. A double row of littleleaf linden trees line the entry drive.

Robert Trent Jones returned to Otter Creek in 1982 to update his design so that the course would remain a challenging test of golf, able to match new club and ball technology. The original 18-hole, 7,258-yard layout has four tee settings to test the ability of the scratch handicapper, yet remains enjoyable for golfers of all skill levels. Ninety-two bunkers protect the bentgrass greens and airways.

In June of 1995, Otter Creek Golf course celebrated the opening of its new 9-hole addition, designed by Rees Jones. The back nine holes reflect the challenge, playability and beauty inherent in the 18 holes designed by Rees' father. The addition showcases a variety of strategically placed grass and sand features, as well as uniquely contoured bentgrass greens, two lakes and Otter Creek. The course is governed by an independent board of directors established by the City of Columbus.

The original golf course and clubhouse were developed and given to the city by Cummins Engine Company, Inc. in June 1964.

Scoreboard (Kevin Roche, 2010)

1965 First Baptist Church

1962 - 1965   3300 Fairlawn Drive

Harry Weese
Jack Hartray, *project manager*
Huong-Lin Swei, *project designer*
Harry Weese and Associates
Chicago, Illinois

Landscape Architect
Dan Kiley
Charlotte, Vermont

Client's statement:
To be "as good as Irwin's (North Christian Church) but half the cost."
    Building Committee, 1961

Architect's statement
(in response to the committee's concern of the unconventional design, materials and perceived 'showcase' design):
"Subjective statements such as 'showcase' reveal a lack of understanding as to the basic simplicity of the concept, essentially exposed structure in simple spaces, two of them with high ceilings. No frills, no finish."
    Harry Weese, July 1963

The predominant silhouette of the two-story building on the hill are two steeply pitched A-frame slate roofs, one smaller than the other, that sit on a brick base. Both roofs at one end have a brick wall that extends above the roof, one with a singular round opening for a bell, which designates this as a place of worship. The two forms are the sanctuary and the chapel, which along with a fellowship hall and offices on the upper level are organized around an internal courtyard. The lower level consists of Sunday school classrooms. The original design was to be concrete walls and wood shingles, but were redesigned in brick and slate shingle for a cost savings.

The main congregational entry is approached by a drive up the hill to a T-shaped opening in a brick wall across a bridge over a moat-like space that brings light to the lower level. The narthex is a low ceiling space which creates a sense of humility before ascending stairs into the high-pitched volume of the sanctuary. The sanctuary is essentially windowless except for the vertical skylights at the front, which highlight a "pierced" brick wall that screens the choir, organ and baptistry behind and narrow glazed openings between the roof overhang and the brick walls. The symmetry of the exposed wood frame structure with wood plank ceiling is contrasted with the asymmetry of the off-center location of the aisle, communion table and pulpit. A centrally suspended wood cross provides a focal point in the random pattern of the brick wall. The building continues to serve its congregation, with only minor modifications completed to the original design for accessibility, lighting or mechanical systems.

Located northeast of downtown, the church is part of a 1960s residential development with W.D. Richards Elementary School across the street and the Par 3 golf course.

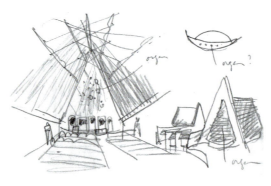

National Historic Landmark, 2000

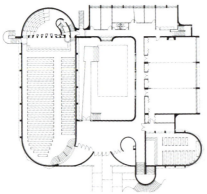

Floor Plan

50

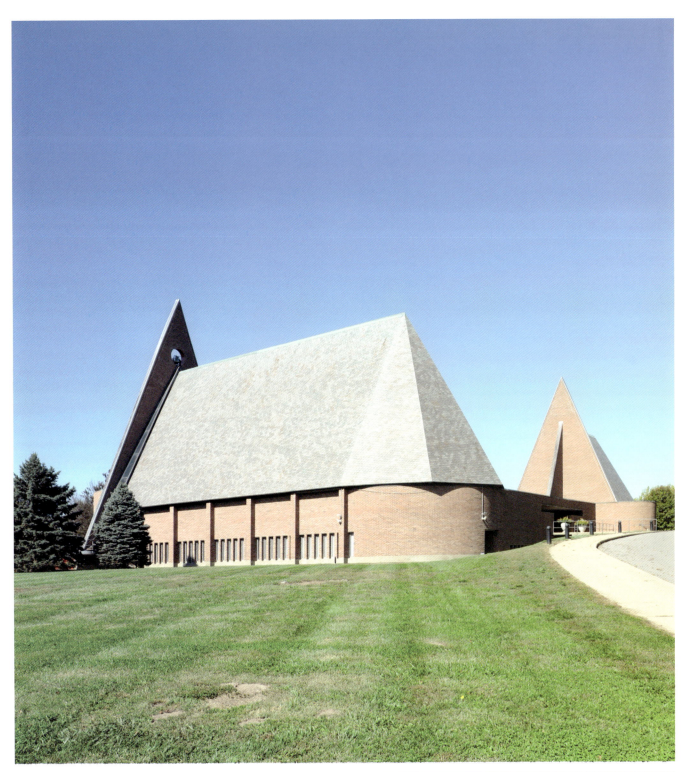

1965 W.D. Richards Elementary School

3311 Fairlawn Drive

Edward Larrabee Barnes
Edward Larrabee Barnes Associates
New York, New York

Landscape Architect
Dan Kiley
Charlotte, Vermont

1997 Addition

John M.Y. Lee
Michael Timchula Architects
New York, New York
Edward Larrabee Barnes, *design consultant*

W. D. Richards Elementary School features bold sloping roofs forming serrated silhouettes. The distinctive high spine of this building is created by the set of four 28-foot high clerestories above the multi-purpose gymnasium/cafeteria in the center of the school. There are parallel corridors on each side of the center room, and smaller clerestories in each classroom.

The purpose of these saw-toothed roofs with skylights is to provide maximum natural studio-type lighting and additional wall space in the classrooms. Each of the six grades are housed in a three-room cluster. Each room has its own outside exit opening onto small plaza areas. The roof silhouette and small courts break down the scale of this large structure into the appearance of a small village. Porthole windows in the classroom doors and other appointments are at child height. Wings forming the entry terrace accommodate the kindergarten area on one side, offices and library on the other. The front entrance of the school, facing west, opens onto a recessed terrace planted with magnolia trees.

The addition includes nine classrooms, a library and computer laboratory, a cafeteria, loading dock facilities and a secondary courtyard with an entrance and bus turn-around for kindergarten and first-grade children. The new classroom design is similar to the older building.

The elementary school is named for William Dalbert Richards (1884-1957), a native of Bartholomew County, who served as teacher and principal in the Columbus elementary schools for 45 years.

Original and addition architect's fees paid by
The Cummins Foundation
Architecture Program

1967 Four Seasons Retirement Center

1901 Taylor Road

Norman Fletcher
The Architects Collaborative (TAC)
Cambridge, Massachusetts

Four Seasons is a retirement community with assisted living, memory care and skilled nursing care. Located on 25 acres of landscaped grounds, there are 78 residential one-level style apartments with vaulted ceilings, large windows, private patio, bath and kitchen. Every apartment opens into a corridor connecting the 12 wings, each of which has a lounge area. Transom windows at the end of each corridor provide natural light.

Centrally located in the complex is an A-framed brick and shingle chapel, peaked with a skylight and bell housing. The interior is mystic with natural light streaming through stained glass above the low perimeter brick walls, washing up the wood ceiling to the bright light of the skylight. The chapel is internally connected to the main entry, which also includes a beauty and barber shop, gift shop, activity studio, library, branch bank, dining areas, recreation lounge and a health-care center with 83 beds. The spacious dining area is located under a large skylight that provides a pleasant atmosphere, including natural interior plantings.

Architect's fees paid by
The Cummins Foundation
Architecture Program

1967 Lincoln Elementary School

1965 - 1967   750 Fifth Street   now Columbus Signature Academy - Lincoln Campus

Gunnar Birkerts
Harold Van Dine, *associate design architect*
Gunnar Birkerts and Associates
Birmingham, Michigan

Landscape Architects
Johnson, Johnson & Roy
Ann Arbor, Michigan

Architect's statement:
"an introverted schoolhouse with a simple brick facade."

"School is not a building...it is an activity... it begins at the sidewalk...it is an educational area...designed to stimulate, challenge or arouse curiosity."
    Gunnar Birkerts

Mrs. Lyndon B. Johnson,
wife of the President of the United States,
on her "Crossroads U.S.A." tour, commemorated her visit to Columbus by dedicating a plaque at the entrance to the school.
    September 1967

American Institute of Architects (AIA)
Honor Award, 1968

Architect's fees paid by
The Cummins Foundation
Architecture Program

Lincoln Elementary School's design is a simple architectural form: a square within a circle. The two-story building is depressed a half-level below ground and encircled with a low retaining wall and a ring of littleleaf linden trees. The play area for the younger children is within this circle, close to the school. The main playground, for the older children, is outside the circle and to the north end of the block, which is bordered with grassy earth berms on four sides, serving as bunkers between the school and streets.

The school is a building within a building. In the center is the multi-purpose room constructed of tongue-and-groove birch walls with laminated wood beams and columns. The "outer-building" is constructed of brick and concrete. From the second-floor corridor, students can look over a parapet topped with narrow, slanted glass windows into the central room below. Corridors surround the multi-purpose room on both levels, with two-story light wells on one side and doorways leading into carpeted classrooms and into special purpose rooms on the other side. Two roof systems are joined by a three foot wide clerestory, or skylight, on all sides of the building, infusing natural light into the central room and the corridors. The concrete and brick structure is highly energy efficient because of the minimal perimeter and innovative fenestration.

In 2001, Gunnar Birkerts designed a triangular shaped addition, that was not completed.

In 2008 the Lincoln Elementary School was transformed into the Columbus Signature Academy, the first K-12 Project-Based Learning magnet school in the nation. Students work collaboratively using technology to solve authentic problems and create real-world projects.

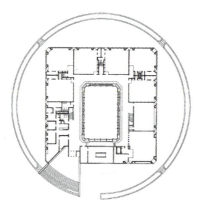

Floor Plan

1968 Fire Station No. 4

1966 - 1968

4730 E. 25th Street

Robert Venturi
Venturi & Rauch
Philadelphia, Pennsylvania

Architect's statement:
"...(we) worked hard to make Fire Station No. 4… look like a fire station. We consciously made this inherently civic but modest building, not heroic and original; we made it ordinary, conventional, familiar…representing perhaps how a child would think of it."

"We used conventional elements, at once functional – it is a garage for trucks plus a barracks – and we weren't afraid of brick and colored brick whose pattern aesthetically affected the perception of the final form of the building..."
    Robert Venturi

This simple, crisp and functional building creates an appropriately ordinary, yet distinctive image for the rescue and social activities associated with a community fire station.

The building committee requested an ordinary building that was easy to maintain. The plan is simple, with almost equal space given to the apparatus rooms and the living/storage quarters. By placing the required hose tower in the front and making it semi-circular, it is absorbed into the facade, giving a monumentality to the otherwise small building and reflecting its civic importance. Because the living quarters did not require the same building height as the engine apparatus room, a parapet is applied to the facade to simplify and unify the front, and enhance its scale. The front facade is predominately white-glazed brick that interlocks in a pattern with the plain red brick of the sides and wraps around the corners. The white brick, gold lettering identifying the station, the hose tower, and the flagpole out front all contribute to the building's civic statement. The angled wall at the back of the building allowed for fire engines to drive around the building on the small site, an innovation for fire stations at that time.

Referencing the popularity of modernism, Venturi said that most architects of the time would have designed a building that would have been "monumental more than civic; its relation to its setting, especially that of a small town, would look to be one of bold contrast…the houses around it probably looking meek…"

This was the first public building that was not a school to be supported by the Cummins Foundation Architecture Program.

Architect's fees paid by
The Cummins Foundation
Architecture Program

Floor Plan

1968 Cummins Technical Center

1963 - 1968   1900 McKinley Avenue

Harry Weese
Harry Weese and Associates
Chicago, Illinois

Landscape Architect
Dan Kiley
Charlotte, Vermont

1997 Renovations   Hellmuth, Obata + Kasssabaum (HOK)
Houston, Texas

2012 Renovations   Flad Architects
Atlanta, Georgia

Cummins Technical Center incorporates two connecting buildings, a six-story, window-wall office building for the professional engineering staff and a two-story research and engine testing facility.

Both buildings are constructed of steel, glass and concrete. The research and engine testing facility utilizes modular, pre-cast concrete panels to create the exterior curtain wall, a method used in several other Cummins buildings constructed since 1957. In contrast, the concrete of the six-story office building was poured floor by floor. Oblong pre-cast concrete forms provide sun screening for the glass windows in each floor. The office interior features formed pre-cast concrete which incorporated the mechanical and electrical systems.

The area around the Technical Center has been landscaped with trees, grass, pools and plantings. Dan Kiley also designed the rows of london plane trees lining Central Avenue (Haw Creek Boulevard) and the plantings around the Cummins Columbus Engine Plant and Cummins Health Center across the boulevard.

The Technical Center was renovated in 1997 as the result of a master plan developed by HOK Architects. The former courtyard between the laboratory and test areas was converted to office use for development engineers. Locating additional office space adjacent to the technical areas provided a more interactive environment which visually connects all areas supporting the engine development process. The renovation also provided a training facility, new cafeteria with outdoor dining, team-focused office conversion in the six-level office building, customer presentation center and expanded specialty laboratories.

1969 Bartholomew County Public Library

1963 - 1969   536 Fifth Street   *orginally called* Cleo Rogers Memorial Library

I. M. Pei, design principal
Kenneth D.B. Carruthers, design architect
Robert H. Landsman, project architect
Robert Lyn, interior design
I. M. Pei and Partners
New York, New York

1971   **"Large Arch"** sculpture
Henry Moore, sculptor
Much Hadham, Hertfordshire, England

1987 Addition   **James K. Paris**
Architect Group, Inc.
Columbus, Indiana

I.M. Pei was hired not only to design a functional building for the county library, but to also assist with the appropriate location within the city. He suggested that it should occupy a space which would be quiet yet dignified, out of the flow of heavy traffic, and be easily accessible to persons of all ages. Its location was selected to create an urban space close to City Hall, which was then located on the corner of Fifth and Franklin Streets. Mr. Pei recommended the closing of Lafayette Street between Fifth and Sixth streets to create the public space across the street from First Christian Church and next to the Irwin house and garden. The plaza would feature a sculpture by Henry Moore, who was recommended by the architect. The open brick paved area has been a place for public concerts and events.

The library building is a brick pavilion with primarily solid walls. The limited tall windows are recessed in deep openings with brick piers at the off-centered main entry. The building corners are expressed with cantilevered parapets and reveal the coffered concrete roof/ceiling structure, predominant on the interior. The austere interiors are spacious with a mezzanine level on the east half, accessed by a sculptured concrete stair. The mezzanine features a skylight above a planter. The coffered ceiling incorporates lighting and acoustical panels. Heating and ventilation is integrated into the window frame system and vertical slots behind brick walls.

The addition was built to the north on a plaza with the original basement level below. The addition is skillfully detailed to match the original building, separated by a sloped skylight to maintain the integrity of the original building.

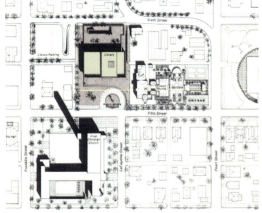

Original Site Plan

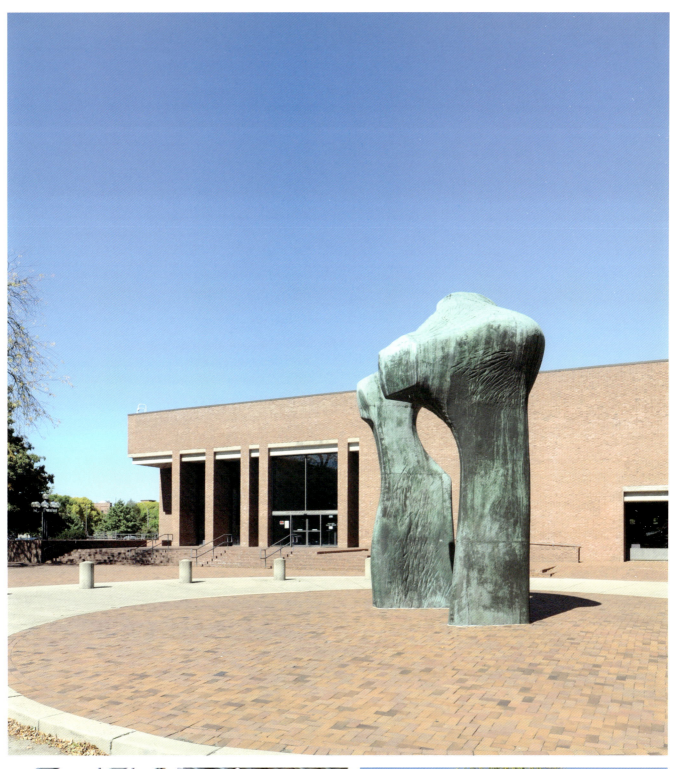

1969   L. Frances Smith Elementary School

4505 Waycross Drive

John M. Johansen
John Johansen, Architect
New Canaan, Connecticut

1997
Addition
& Renovation

John M. Johansen, *design consultant*
Christian M. Johansen, *design architect*
Loeffler, Johansen, Bennett, Architects, P.C.
New Canaan, Connecticut

Architect's statement:
"L. Frances Smith Elementary School utilizes lightweight, colored sheet metal for its peripheral elements... and illustrates my growing interest... in lightness and mobility."
    John M. Johansen

Public comment:
"Not one child disagrees with the design of our, the town's, school building. Just because it is an up-to-date, modern building doesn't mean people must condemn it... Anyone that is disgusted with it, well maybe they had better visit us inside. We, the kids, love it!"
    10 year old student
    at Frances Smith School, 1969

While the brightly colored metal circulation tubes are what make this elementary school unique, it is the distinction between the heavy concrete "fixed" elements (seminar rooms, faculty offices, and carrels) and the lightweight, brightly-colored, sheet metal elements (classrooms and speciality rooms) that radiate out from a central courtyard that make this school design innovative. It was designed to be additive with additional parts, which it was by the architect's son in 1997.

The open spaces within the two core ramps and nodes provide a courtyard and amphitheater for a variety of events. Three new classroom wings are united with a library on top and a play area below. The circulation tubes connect at glass-encased nodes which provide kaleidoscopic views out for the children. The tubes have rounded corners to give children the sensation of being "extruded".

The organization of this school begins with the administration offices and primary classrooms at grade level and ascends to higher levels and upper grades culminating with the media/computer center at the top. The new gymnasium, cafeteria wing and the music and art wings are zoned to operate independently from the rest of the school, providing after-school and community activities when school is not in session.

This school was named in honor of Miss L. Frances Smith (1901-1971), a teacher for 10 years prior to serving as a supervisor of elementary education in Columbus schools for 24 years.

Original and Addition architect's fees paid by
The Cummins Foundation
Architecture Program

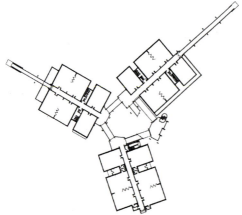

Original Floor Plan

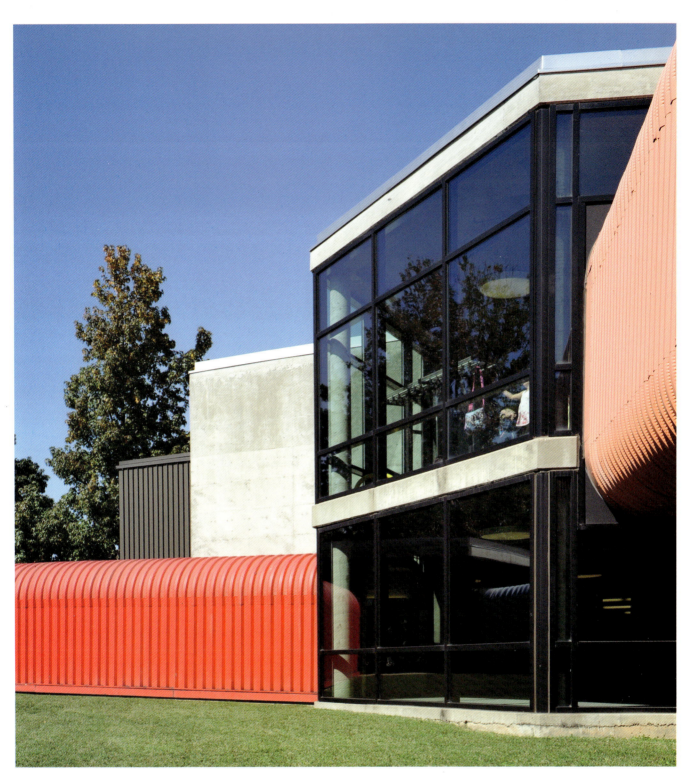

1969 Southside Elementary School

County Road 200 South

originally Southside Junior High

Eliot Noyes
Alan Goldberg, associate architect
Eliot Noyes Architect
New Canaan, Connecticut

Murals
Ivan Chermayeff, Artist
New York, New York

Southside Elementary School appears as a fortress. Its precast concrete exterior is articulated with vertical fins, recessed and slot windows, blank walls and sculptured projecting stairways. The exposed concrete, both outside and inside, provide a low maintenance building and energy conservation.

The austere exterior conceals a surprisingly light-filled interior, with a two-story central commons space topped with a skylight. A large open staircase ties the two floors together, with an overlooking balcony on all sides. The interiors are given warmth with walnut-stained oak woodwork and furniture, as well as carpeted corridors.

The main floor includes a 400-seat dividable auditorium, a gymnasium and a swimming pool, as well as classrooms. The upper level features the library and four clusters of classrooms each with a resource center, small seminar room and smaller conference rooms.

The four projecting concrete stairwells are uniquely naturally lit with clerestory and vertical slot windows. Each has been enlivened with brightly colored abstract murals by Ivan Chermayeff.

To the west of the school is a small concrete and glass power plant which showcased the school boiler. With a donated Cummins generator, the school was intended to be self sufficient, described as a "total energy system". A circular parking lot surrounds this unique structure.

To meet the changing educational needs of the community, the building, formerly a junior high school, was converted to an elementary school in 1983.

Murals commissioned by
Mr. & Mrs. J. Irwin Miller

Architect's fees paid by
The Cummins Foundation
Architecture Program

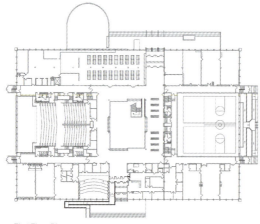

First Floor Plan

1970 U.S. Post Office - Columbus

1965 - 1970   450 Jackson Street

Kevin Roche
John Dinkeloo
Kevin Roche John Dinkeloo and Associates
Hamden, Connecticut

Architect's intention:
Columns fronting the Post Office are reminiscent of the Federal style while at the same time suggesting the open arcades typical of western towns. Reflective glass across the entrance and lobbies provide adequate separation of exterior and interior, yet from the outside creates an illusion of greater space.
Dedication brochure, July 19, 1970

This downtown building is dominated by an arcade made of brown load-bearing tiles, which gives it a civic scale, and is later continued with the arcade of the Cummins Corporate Office Building to the north, also designed by Kevin Roche. The large size of the columns give the one-story building a grand presence. The exposed street structure of the arcade roof is built of cor-ten steel, a self weathering steel. The salt-glazed tile, commonly used in silos, was glazed reddish-brown to match the color of the cor-ten.

On-site visitor parking and the mail truck delivery docks are incorporated into the overall design of the building with tile walls and pylons, a continuation of the tile building walls. The mirrored-glass windows and doors on the front of the building provide interesting reflections. From the inside this glass treatment is transparent. High ceilings lend an air of spaciousness to the entire building.

Locating the Post Office downtown was a commitment to long-range redevelopment plans to restore and retain the city's downtown area.

This project was the first U.S. post office designed by a privately funded architect.

Architect's fees paid by
The Cummins Foundation
Architecture Program

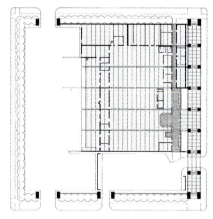

Floor Plan

1971 The Republic

1969 - 1971   333 Second Street

Myron Goldsmith, *design partner*
Jin Kim, *senior designer*
George Larson, *interior designer*
Skidmore, Owings & Merrill (SOM)
Chicago, Illinois

1998 Renovation

Todd Williams
Todd Williams Architect
Columbus, Indiana

Architect's statement:
"The location of the newspaper on the Courthouse Square affirms its position as a force in the life and growth of the community. The building is constructed of steel and glass with the interior layout based on the most efficient flow of work through the building. The interior is highly visible from the street with the press in a prominent location contributing as a powerful sculpture."
    Myron Goldsmith, 1971

Owner's statement:
"The one thing that has stayed constant throughout the years is the impact it (the building) has on our employees. Dad believed that outstanding building design would set a higher bar in the work he expected to be produced from within its walls every day. That continues to be the case today for all of us working here."
    Jeff Brown, fifth generation family newspaper owner, son of Bob Brown
    2012

American Institute of Architects (AIA) Honor Award, 1971

National Historic Landmark, 2012

The simple glass and steel building design was the result of a close working relationship with the fourth generation family newspaper owner Bob Brown and the architect Myron Goldsmith. Together they developed the concept of a modern newspaper plant based on an open interior plan that offered views of the interior workings of the building from the outside. The relationship began with a newspaper building in Franklin, Indiana.

The downtown Columbus design emphasized openness of the newspaper to the community. Located south of the historic Bartholomew County Courthouse, the building is setback from the main street with a double row of trees and a simple grass lawn. The original centerpiece of the design was the yellow offset printing press visible at the front of the building. The press was removed in 1998, with the area renovated to additional office space and a meeting room. Newspaper production was relocated to the new Printing Center.

The single story building is primarily open offices with exposed structural steel and high ceilings that integrate lights, acoustical decking and fire sprinklers. The interior is painted white, including the custom designed workstations. The extensive use of glass provides lots of natural light and views. The walls are accented with contemporary art or artifacts of the newspaper's original building.

The Republic was designated a National Historic Landmark in 2012, the seventh modern building in Columbus to receive that status. The Republic was described as "an exceptional work of modern architecture and one of the best examples of the work of Myron Goldsmith, a general partner in the firm Skidmore, Owings & Merrill, and a highly respected architect, architectural theorist, writer, and educator."

Original Floor Plan

photo courtesy of The Republic

1972 301 Washington St.

301 Washington Street — Entry facade and interiors

Alexander Girard
Sante Fe. New Mexico

2011
Interior Renovation

David Force
Force Design
Columbus, Indiana

Architect's statement:
"It is all very severe, very quiet."
Alexander Girard, 1975

301 Washington Street was the "neutral" office of J. Irwin Miller, who was the President/Chairman of Cummins Engine Company, President of Irwin Union Bank and the Irwin-Sweeney-Miller Foundation, as well as other business interests and national associations.

The Victorian building was originally built in 1881 by Joseph Irwin as a dry good store, and eventually became Irwin's Bank. Alexander Girard, the interior designer for the Miller House, was also an architect. He was responsible for the facade renovation including the recessed entry with the white ceramic tile walls, the globe light fixtures in the coffered ceiling and the distinctive projecting gold entry vestibule with side doors.

Simplicity of design is reflected in the remodeled interiors that feature rounded corners, clean lines and attention to detail including light switches hidden behind curtains. The second floor offices showcase strong lines and very subtle colors. The ceilings are a custom egg crate with uniform lighting, and the carpet was custom designed with a linear pattern. The doors are sliding wood panels. The custom open screen separated the stair and the second floor reception area. J. Irwin Miller's private office features a built-in desk and credenza, a horizontal wood wall accent with storage behind, a hidden television set and a recessed wall clock. The fireplace burned only coal. The office chairs were custom produced bronze by furniture maker Herman Miller.

In 2011, Cummins purchased the building and renovated the interiors for additional downtown office space. The first floor entry and second floor private office of J. Irwin Miller have been preserved and are accessible for public tours offered by the Columbus Area Visitors Center.

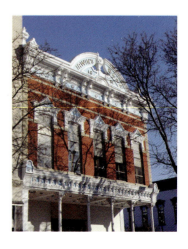

Original First Floor Plan, 1975

1972 Columbus East High School

230 South Marr Road

Ehrman Mitchell
Romaldo Giurgola
Mitchell-Giurgola Architects
Philadelphia, Pennsylvania

1998 Gym Addition	Mitchell-Giurgola Architects Philadelphia, Pennsylvania
2011 Addition & Renovation	CSO Architects Indianapolis, Indiana

Architectural statement:
"Columbus East is a reconciliation of disparate elements, both of its functional program and its community context. Its taut character reminds us that, for all the talk about "complexity and contradiction," there can be a still higher relationship - "complexity and complementarity."
Architectural Record, 1976

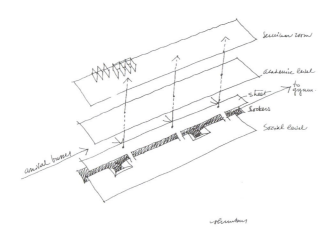

American Institute of Architects (AIA)
Honor Award, 1975

Architect's fees paid by
The Cummins Foundation
Architecture Program

The architects were challenged by the school administration to design a high school building to fit a flexible program. The heart of the building is the two-story gallery level which includes a commons and cafeteria, with a wall of glass opening onto a terrace. The main floor, which has a half-wall above the commons area and a lower-level corridor, includes the offices, library, bookstore and five instruction rooms for large groups.

The second floor is totally academic, containing resource centers, laboratories and classrooms. The open area on the second floor enhances the concept that exposure to other subjects will generate wider interests. On the third floor are a series of small classrooms for about 15 students each. The classrooms are directly above the resource centers for ease in transporting instructional materials. The school program emphasizes individual study with faculty guidance and includes traditional classrooms. A 900-seat auditorium, used for a variety of community purposes, is at the north end of the school, and a 4,200-seat gymnasium is at the south end. Special features include a swimming pool, planetarium, a specially equipped industrial arts wing, a greenhouse, a TV studio and an animal room for science classes. Outdoor tennis courts are nearby.

A second gymnasium was constructed in 1998 to accommodate the growth in physical education programs, girls' and boys' sports and other extracurricular activities. The 2011 addition and renovation enclosed the open courtyard and "relocated" the original monumental brick entry.

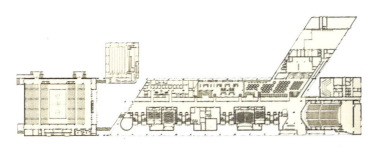

Original Floor Plan

1972 Mt. Healthy Elementary School

12150 South State Road 58

Hugh Hardy, *principal design architect*
Michael Kaplan, *project architect*
Hardy Holzman Pfeiffer Associates
New York, New York

2002 Addition

Nolan Bingham
Paris Bingham Partnership
Columbus, Indiana

Architect's statement:
"The building was planned to reflect the future, which is actually a combination of the present and the past, with the best parts of both."
  Hugh Hardy, 1972

Based upon the educational philosophy of team teaching and individual student development, this was the first open classroom plan school for Bartholomew County. The architect organized the plan around two basic concepts: the open plan and the superimposition of grids.

Three multi-level "classroom" clusters provide primary, upper primary and intermediate teaching areas, featuring a two-story space topped with diagonal saw-toothed clerestory windows and large industrial windows which have since been infilled with metal panels for energy conservation. Different areas in the clusters are architecturally distinguished with low walls, changes in floor levels, movable furniture, natural and artificial lighting, and a variety of juxtaposed materials, finishes and colors. Exposed structural and mechanical systems are painted primary colors.

A diagonal path, delineated by a variegated carpet, ties the open clusters and the enclosed gymnasium, offices and support spaces together. Because the volumes of enclosure are not congruent with the plan, movement through the building offers a spatial variety and a sense of discovery.

The school board requested a "seamless" addition in 2002, which added a new entry, administrative offices, meeting rooms and an enlarged gymnasium/gathering space, as well as some remodeling. This school is the first rural Bartholomew County school built under the Cummins Engine Foundation Architecture Program.

Architect's fees paid by
The Cummins Foundation
Architecture Program

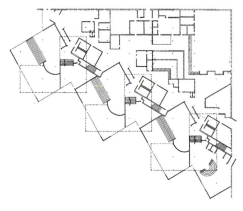

Original Floor Plan

1972 Par 3 Golf Course Clubhouse

Fairlawn at Par 3 Drive

Brewster (Bruce) Adams
Bruce Adams, designer
New Haven, Connecticut

This clubhouse, designed to be a good neighbor to the nearby First Baptist Church and W.D. Richards Elementary School, was built of wood shingle roof and cedar siding. It includes a pro shop, lounge, restrooms and storage space.

The simplicity of this building's form is dominated by the large pitched roof, which is then articulated with a skewed plan, an elongated eye brow window and an arcade/loggia overlooking the golf course. A cube on a pole with super graphics created a simple identity. The "knuckle" of the skewed plan creates a covered entry from the parking lot to the golf course. A practice green and existing trees blend this natural structure into the landscape.

Par 3 is an excellent facility for young golfers learning the game, and for adults of all ages enjoying leisure play. The 45 acre golf course was originally constructed in 1965, beautifully landscaped with crabapple, blue spruce, scotch pine and pin oak trees.

Architect's fees paid by
The Cummins Foundation
Architecture Program

1972 Mental Health Center

1969 - 1972   2975 Lincoln Park Drive   *originally* Quinco Consulting Center

James Stewart Polshek
W. Todd Springer, *associate*
Dimitre Linard, *associate*
James McCullar
James Stewart Polshek and Associates
New York, New York

The building's decisive design element is that it spans Haw Creek. On one bank is Columbus Regional Hospital's main campus; on the other is a city park. The site was chosen for its serene setting, conducive to the services it provides – individual, family and group therapy for a variety of mental health disorders.

The two-story building is organized with two offset rectangular plans, and a skylighted two-story lounge located at the broad middle section. The main entry is across a concrete bridge. The building's ends are solid concrete walls that cantilever over the glass entry with a single recessed window above. The west portion of the building is itself a bridge, supported with concrete piers. Above the creek the building features generous horizontal windows, with unique angled glass panels on the top floor creating a skylight effect for the individual rooms within.

The first floor has facilities for crisis intervention and an adolescent partial hospitalization program. The second floor houses an 18-bed inpatient mental health unit that serves adult through geriatric patients and a dayroom facility that houses a partial hospitalization program for geriatric outpatients. This facility and its services are largely the result of the efforts of Lowell Engelking, a local business leader, philanthropist and the first president of the Bartholomew County Mental Health Association.

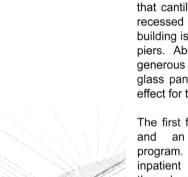
Axonometric Plan

Architect's fees paid by
The Cummins Foundation
Architecture Program

Rendering

1972 Irwin Office Building

1966 - 1972   500 Washington Street (Jackson Street)   *originally* Irwin Union Bank & Trust Company Office Building

Kevin Roche
Kevin Roche John Dinkeloo and Associates (KRJDA)
Hamden, Connecticut

1969 Expansion

Park and Bank Drive-Thru
Kevin Roche
Kevin Roche John Dinkeloo and Associates
Hamden, Connecticut

Landscape Architect
Jack Curtis
Monroe, Connecticut

1989 Expansion

Building Expansion
Kevin Roche John Dinkeloo and Associates
Hamden, Connecticut

2012 Renovations

Exterior Renovations
Todd Williams
Todd Williams and Associates
Columbus, Indiana

Interior Modifications
Axis Architects
Indianapolis, Indiana

Architectural Advisors
Kevin Roche
Philip Kinsella
KRJDA

The simple three-story office building is an addition to the Irwin Union Bank designed by Eero Saarinen. The predominately glass building thematically relates to the original building, connected with a glass corridor/galleria that was originally a public pass through. The full height southern exposed galleria overlooks a park and bank drive-through that had been completed several years prior.

To reduce the heat gain in the enclosed galleria, the original green tinted glass featured laminated panels with a mirrored coating creating horizontal strips. The glass was replaced in 2012 with the horizontal strips composed of ceramic frit dots. The northern facade featured an open metal trellis over a raised entry patio, that mimics the sloped profile of the galleria, on which wisteria and trumpet vines grow.

The building interior features exposed steel trusses, due to the low floor-to-floor height to match scale of the adjacent 19th century buildings. The open floors are kept column free with long-span trusses and by placing the building support rooms (stairs, elevators and restrooms) in brick enclosures at both ends of the building. The grey brick was the same brick originally selected by Saarinen to face the side of the adjacent building.

In 1989 the bank was enlarged further by renovating two buildings to the north with cast iron columns and glass Victorian facades. Kevin Roche directed the renovation of these buildings, one of which was designed by prolific local architect Charles F. Sparrell.

Cummins purchased the building in 2011 and now houses additional downtown offices within. The interior has been renovated with open office areas and a variety of enclosed meeting rooms to encourage collaboration.

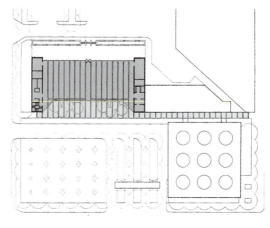

Site Plan

1973 Cummins Health Center

605 Cottage Avenue *originally called* **Cummins Occupational Health Association (COHA)**

Hugh Hardy
Malcolm Holzman
Norman Pfeiffer
Michael Ross, *project architect*
Hardy Holzman Pfeiffer Associates
New York, New York

Landscape Architect
Dan Kiley
Charlotte, Vermont

Architectural statement:
The design "exposes routine medical functions to both patient and technician which relieves the tedium of clinical work and the anxiety of patients."
AIA Honor Award, 1976

This facility is an alternative approach to industrial health care design, providing occupational and preventive health services. Departing from the traditional concept of a clinic, the facility has been designed with an abundance of glass and few interior walls. A small building of only 21,000 square feet, with three floors connected with open ramps and stairways.

The health center's design is based on a configuration of open, semi-open and closed spaces defined by two overlapping geometric grids. Closed private activities are set around the building's perimeter in the outer grid, finished in black glass, which is opaque during daylight. Open public activities are set within the internal grid, whose edges delineate separate public and staff circulations; these paths are outlined above by skylights. A large central waiting space, which leads to all medical functions, is bisected by two gently sloping circulation ramps that connect the three half-levels of the building, with circular seating pods placed throughout.

The design utilized standard building materials in novel ways. The red corrugated metal siding entry wall is supported by roof trusses installed vertically and the curved continuous skylights are constructed of typical greenhouse components. Vertically ribbed concrete block provide interior texture. Brightly colored mechanical and structural systems accentuate the building's various layers inside. The surrounding landscape can be seen from throughout the center, and at night the building's transparent walls make the interior clearly visible from the outside. The three-story building exhibits a sophisticated design with a low profile so it does not overwhelm the neighboring small houses.

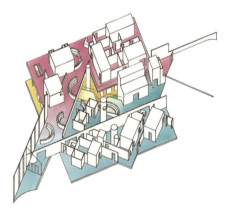

American Institute of Architects (AIA)
Honor Award, 1976

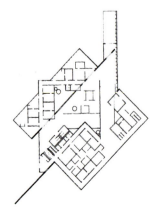

Floor Plan

1973 Columbus Midrange Engine Plant

1970 - 1973   2725 W. County Road 450 S.   *originally called* Cummins Engine Company Sub-Assembly Plant

Kevin Roche
Kevin Roche John Dinkeloo and Associates (KRJDA)
Hamden, Connecticut

Landscape Architect
Dan Kiley
Charlotte, Vermont

1991   Facility updated for midrange engine assembly

To preserve the surrounding wooded site, this 13 acre building is depressed into a clearing and features parking on the roof. The main floor of the building is actually two levels with the manufacturing floor three feet lower than the office areas, which surrounds it on three sides. There are three roof top glass entry structures, two are secured employee entries with stairs and escalators, the other is a visitors entry with an elevator. The prominent northern glass structure was originally a high-bay warehousing area.

The layout of the plant provides all occupants with a view of the outside. In the middle of the manufacturing area is a landscaped courtyard completely surrounded by glass. Light and views of the outside environment are facilitated with a slanted glass roof at the cafeteria, located in the southwest corner of the building.

One of the main goals in the building design was the preservation and enhancement of the environment for those using the facility. As a result, special attention was given to creating an environmentally controlled system of air, noise and water pollution control devices which surpassed industry standards at the time. This factory was proclaimed a prototype of future factory buildings in the early 1970s.

Since the manufacturing and assembly areas were designed to be highly flexible and efficient, the original component machining and assembly equipment were easily removed to allow assembly lines utilizing computerization and robotic systems to build the midrange engines, without impacting the building's architecture.

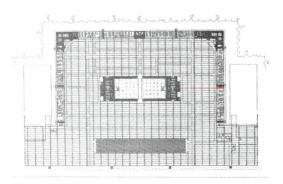

Floor Plan

1973 Fodrea Community School

2775 Illinois Street   now Columbus Signature Academy - Fodrea Campus

Paul Kennon, *design architect*
Truitt Garrison, *assistant design architect*
Caudill Rowlett Scott (CRS)
Houston, Texas

2010 Renovation   CSO Architects
Indianapolis, Indiana

In a process that CRS called "squatting", the architects asked kids, parents, faculty and administration what they thought the school should be. "The kids wanted slides, ramps, robot teachers, push-button desks, waterbeds and even a tunnel of love..."
Progressive Architecture, 1974

This "people-centered" school is one of the first in the country to be designed as a community center as well as a school. It is the third Columbus school designed in the open classroom concept for team teaching, with three "learning areas," two kindergarten areas and several multi-purpose areas. It offers elementary education, recreation and community-civic organization space.

The architects incorporated suggestions made by the children who attended the school and by members of the community at a series of open meetings. One feature of the school is a public concourse leading to an open courtyard, originally planted with trees, in the center of the school. This area is still accessible to visitors. An enclosed two story Materials Resource Center occupies a third of the central concourse, bounded with two levels of classrooms. The open classrooms have been enclosed with the renovation.

The predominately white exterior, with prefabricated insulated metal panels, features three half-round entries highlighted with primary colors and super graphic numbers. The exposed structure uses a "unistrut" space frame with metal deck supported on concrete columns with inverted pyramidal connections. Mechanical systems and lighting are exposed in the interiors.

This school was named for three sisters, Miss Hazel Fodrea, Miss Bess Fodrea and Mrs. Mabel Fodrea Jordan, who taught a total of 84 years in community schools.

In 2010 the Fodrea School was transformed into the Columbus Signature Academy, the first K-12 Project-Based Learning magnet school in the nation. Students work collaboratively using technology to solve authentic problems and create real-world projects.

Architect's fees paid by
The Cummins Foundation
Architecture Program

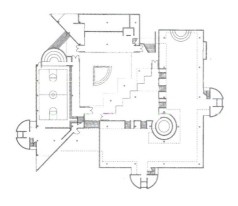

Floor Plan

1974 State Street Branch Bank

State and Mapleton Street branch

originally Irwin Union Bank

Paul Kennon, *design principal*
Caudill Rowlett Scott (CRS)
Houston, Texas

Landscape Architect
Dan Kiley
Charlotte, Vermont

Located on State Street, this branch bank was an enlarged facility with drive-up teller service from the small bank building (now a Flower shop) across the street designed by Harry Weese in 1961.

This bank features two parallel two-story brick walls that conceal mechanical equipment and office space in between. The original banking hall was enclosed by a sloped glass structure with tinted glass. The entries at both ends are projecting glass vestibules. The five drive-through lanes are covered with an exposed structural space frame with metal deck and bubble skylights.

The trapezoidal site is enhanced with trees and landscaping which give the building a mini-parklike setting. The street front is layered with a formal row of trees, similar to the downtown bank by Saarinen, while the back is more natural.

1978 AT&T Switching Center

Seventh and Franklin Streets   *originally* Indiana Bell Telephone Switching Center

Paul Kennon, *design architect*
Jay Bauer, *assistant design architect*
Caudill Rowlett Scott (CRS)
Houston, Texas

Associate Architects
Boots-Smith & Associates
Indianapolis, Indiana

Architectural comment:
"...a delightful whimsical solution to the use of mirrored glass."
    AIA Honor Award, 1980

Architect's statement:
"For my father, (the trellis) was an integral part of the building, the idea was central to the heart and soul of the building."
    Kevin Kennon (son of Paul Kennon), 2010

American Institute of Architects (AIA)
Honor Award, 1980

Distinctive for its mirrored glass facade and its primary colored accents, the basically unoccupied building houses electronic equipment for the telephone company. Originally a three-story brick building, Indiana Bell commissioned Paul Kennon to add an addition and create a new cohesive design on a transitional site, joining the business district and one of the community's older, but viable residential areas.

The design solution was to unify the existing building and the new addition by encasing both in a skin of reflective glass. Reflecting the neighboring building, the resulting "non-building" was also originally screened with two freestanding vertical space-frame trellis structures intended to be covered with wisteria and climbing greenery behind a row of pear trees on the street fronts.

Giant yellow, orange, red and blue "crayons" or "organ pipes" on the west alley side of the building provide a colorful accent, and have been an iconic image of the modern architecture of Columbus. They are actually color-coded functional stacks for the building's heating, ventilation and air conditioning system: blue for air intake, red for exhaust, orange for diesel intake and yellow for diesel exhaust. Building service entry doors and other exhaust elements are also accented with primary colors.

The majority of the trellis structure and the pear trees, which were an integral part of the original design concept, have unfortunately been removed due to excessive birds and their droppings on the sidewalk below. The reflective glass is still effective in making the building disappear into its surroundings. The modern building is an example of the community's commitment to design excellence, even with a typically mundane functional facility.

1981 Columbus City Hall
123 Washington Street

Edward Charles Bassett, *principal architect*
Skidmore, Owings & Merrill (SOM)
San Francisco, California

Client's comment:
"Each major building makes a lasting statement about a community, especially its people and their standards. Fortunately, Columbus has a rich heritage of high standards and a concern for the well-being of our citizens. City Hall strengthens that tradition."
Nancy Ann Brown, Mayor, 1981

Architect's fees paid by
The Cummins Foundation
Architecture Program

The Columbus City Hall creates an imposing civic presence for a relatively small 60,000 square foot building. The diagonal front of this right triangle building bisects its full block site and creates a strong visual relationship with Washington Street, Second Street and the neighboring Bartholomew County Courthouse. City Hall's main entry, reached by a series of broad steps, invites members of the community and visitors to come inside. Two brick clad cantilevered beams create a distinctive entry to a semi-circular forecourt, bordered with a window wall of glass. Indiana limestone is used for the exterior base of the building, with the upper two floors encased in brick.

Behind the glass façade, a two-story gallery reveals the upper floor balcony, which is reached by staircases at either end of the main floor. These two floors contain the city government departments, conference rooms, the Council Chamber on the upper level, and a Meeting Hall on the court level. Large louvered oak doors separate the offices from the gallery. The ground floor, with its entrance on the east side of the building, houses the city Police Department. Interior decorations include Amish quilts, photographs of Columbus buildings, renderings of downtown storefronts designed by Alexander Girard, murals of legendary residents, commissioned paintings by Robert Indiana and William T. Wiley, and a bust of Christopher Columbus. The Wiley painting "History-Mystery" is stretched on the tympanum of the Council Chamber.

Landscape plantings include littleleaf linden trees in the efficient parking areas to the south and east, european beech and a sugar maple tree on the front lawn. Shrubs, hedges and boston ivy complete the plantings.

Floor Plan

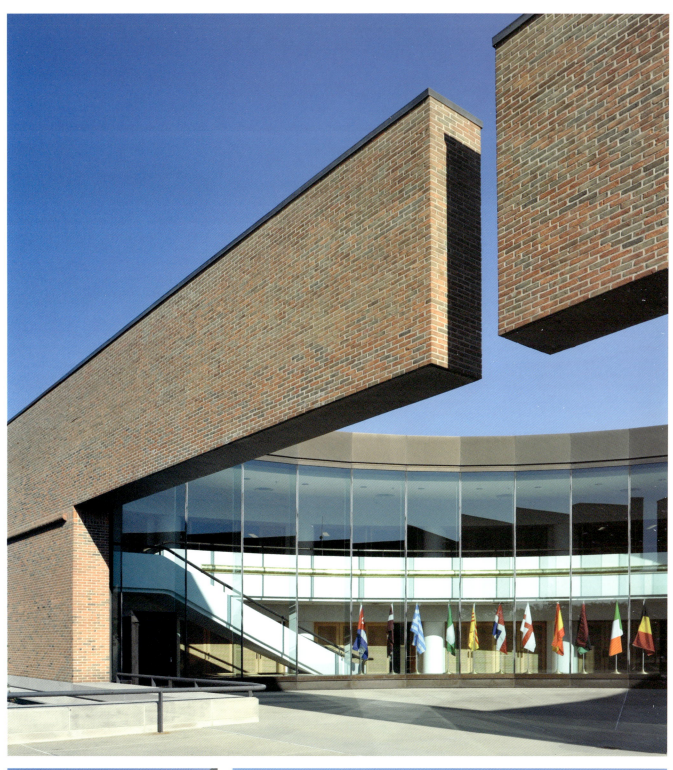

1982 CERAland Recreation Center
3989 South 525 East

Harry Roth
Roth and Moore Architects
New Haven, Connecticut

CERAland is a beautiful 345 acre recreational park located southeast of Columbus, with outdoor sport and recreation facilities, a stocked lake, an outdoor aquatic center, a campground, and an indoor sport and fitness center. The indoor recreational facility, designed by Harry Roth, contains two full-size gymnasiums for basketball and volleyball, a one-ninth mile running track, an exercise room with a full range of weight equipment, locker rooms, meeting rooms and offices.

The predominant architectural features are the two barrel vaulted roofs with aluminum standing seam roofing recalling local farm buildings, supported by beautiful wood bow trusses in each gymnasium. An indoor second floor jogging track runs around the perimeter of each gymnasium and through the support space in between, which is expressed with a sloped skylight and windows to bring in natural lighting.

The interiors are otherwise windowless to control light levels and provide energy conservation. The predominant building material on the exterior and interior is poured-in-place concrete, providing a durable and low maintenance material. The surrounding exterior berms provide additional energy conservation and structural support for the trusses. The gray concrete on the interior is warmed by the wood structure and the maple playing floors. The exterior uses redwood siding for the non-load bearing end walls of the barrel vault. The main entry is highlighted by an arched opening and a recessed loggia with a glass block wall on both sides of the glass entry.

Originally operated by and for employees of Cummins Engine Company and their families, today CERAland is open to everyone with membership.

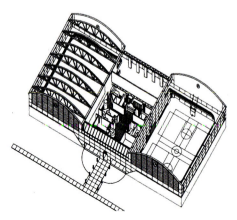

Axonometric Plan

1982 Clifty Creek Elementary School

1978 - 1982   4625 East 50 North

Richard Meier, *design principal*
Gerald Gurland, *assistant design principal*
Philip Babb, *associate-in-charge*
Richard Meier and Partners
New York, New York

1997
Addition
& Renovation

Peter Stamberg
Paul Aferiat
Stamberg Aferiat Architecture
New York, New York

Architect's statement:
"A ship-like school on a sea of grass."
        Richard Meier

The school board wanted fresh design ideas and traditional classrooms, instead of the open classroom concept of previous Columbus schools. Consequently, Richard Meier was selected as the architect since he had never designed a school before.

Located on a sloping 22 acre site, the three-story classroom wing connects with a centrally located library and a two-story support building on top of the hill, containing the administrative offices, cafeteria, gymnasium, art and music classrooms. The double-height, north lit library features Meier's signature glass curtain wall and open ramps, as well as a piano-curved story-telling balcony.

Renowned for his white porcelain panel buildings, Meier instead selected white glazed and gray concrete block for a durable and low maintenance exterior, as well as white framed windows and glass block. The classrooms are paired together with a movable partition and there is a glass enclosed activity room where students can work by themselves while still under the supervision of the classroom teacher. The interiors were originally all white, since Meier believed "color comes from the way light comes into the building...and serves as a canvas for the children's paintings...Kids add color and make each classroom different."

The addition provided more classrooms to the three-story wing, matching the original building and replacing the curved end wall that gave the building a ship-like character. The addition added an elevator, additional restrooms, teacher prep rooms and a sunscreen for the library curtainwall for energy efficiency in the courtyard. The renovation also added color to the building interiors and exterior.

Original and Addition architect's fees paid by
The Cummins Foundation
Architecture Program

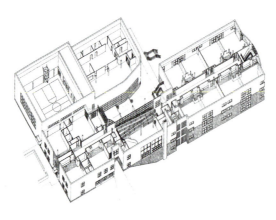

Axonometric Plan - original design

1982 Sycamore Place

222 Sycamore Street

Charles Gwathmey, *design principal*
Jacob Alspector, *associate-in-charge*
Gwathmey Siegel & Associates Architects
New York, New York

Architect's statement:
The design intention "was to transform the image of subsidized housing by making a building with presence, that was contextual and responsive to the inhabitants, while simultaneously establishing a 'sense of place.' "
Gwathmey Siegel & Associates

Sycamore Place is a HUD-subsidized public housing project for seniors. Located on 2nd Street, four blocks east of City Hall, it is surrounded by a mixture of commercial buildings and modest houses. At three stories, it is the tallest building in the area, but recedes due to its muted color and varied form.

With 24 one-bedroom apartments, the building plan stairsteps back accommodating a private balcony for each unit avoiding views into the adjacent bedroom. The staggered corridor also provides privacy at the entries and features natural daylight at the ends. The balconies and sense of privacy are unique for public housing, avoiding an institutional feel. The building also includes a double-height community room, a kitchen, a lounge, a laundry and a beauty salon. The entry features a photomural by Elliot Kaufman.

The wood framed building is enclosed with low maintenance horizontal cedar siding stained gray, accented with white framed windows and trim. The asphalt shingled roof forms are a simple gable, with a half-gable shed roof expression on the east end. The main entry is off a covered drive-through which doubles as an entry plaza. A circular seating area in the front features a sculptured concrete sundial. The site has been landscaped with a variety of trees including Bradford Pears, Douglas Firs, Red maples, Littleleaf Linden and Honey locust. A thousand daffodils were planted amongst a bed of periwinkle.

Architect's fees paid by
The Cummins Foundation
Architecture Program

Site / First Floor Plan

1984 Cummins Corporate Office Building

1977 - 1984
original design 1974

500 Jackson Street

Kevin Roche
John Kinsella, *project architect*
Kevin Roche John Dinkeloo and Associates
Hamden, Connecticut

Landscape Architect
Jack Curtis
Meg Storrow
Monroe, Connecticut

"Exploded Engine"
Rudolph de Harak, *sculptor*
New York, New York

Architect's statement:
"For the new headquarters the company was looking to create an efficient, flexible environment where work space followed the needs of the employee rather than his or her rank."
    Kevin Roche

Client's comment:
"You try to create an environment in which people will feel like doing their best work. You can have the best environment in the world, but if you have an authoritarian management it won't work. The environment can support the human climate that you're trying to create, and this is one in which I guess everybody is essential to the process."
    J. Irwin Miller

Cummins corporate headquarters is a one-story building with a mezzanine level that occupies three blocks in downtown Columbus. The zigzag plan configuration of the office building interacts with a parklike setting of exterior spaces, entries and visitor parking. The east side is defined with a trellis structure that defines the green space and features the four story historic Cerealine building, which produced one of the world's first dry breakfast cereals. The restored and renovated red brick building now houses the employee cafeteria, surrounded by a glass addition and a pond.

The main office building is primarily cast-in-place white octagonal columns with infilled precast concrete spandrels and narrow windows, to provide noise and sun control, as well as energy conservation. The interior spandrels are faced with mirrors to create a feeling of expansion, in which one also reflects the exterior. The northern walls have larger expanses of glass to visually connect to the exterior park setting. Natural light is further introduced to the interior through continuous roof skylights.

The original building design began from the inside to create a better work environment. The "two-story" high open office space is spacious, with enclosed office and conference rooms internally located, with large glass walls, providing both natural lighting and interaction with the open office.

The arcade of columns relates to the portico of the Post Office to the south, designed by Kevin Roche in 1970, and the defined "public" park setting relates to the original civic concepts of First Christian Church by Eliel Saarinen. The southeast corner of the building is cut away to provide a covered visitor entrance. The lobby houses the Corporate Office Building Museum featuring their diesel engines and cars with their engines.

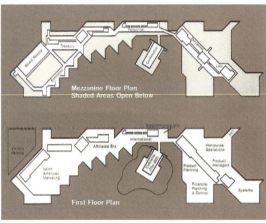

Floor Plans

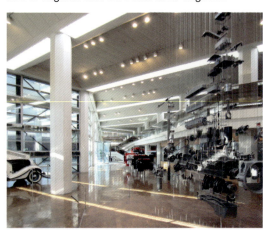

1984 Pence Place Apartments

Pence Place

Charles Gwathmey, *design principal*
Jacob Alspector, *associate-in-charge*
Gwathmey Siegel & Associates Architects
New York, New York

1999 Renovation — Gwathmey Siegel & Associates Architects
New York, New York

Pence Place is the second HUD-subsidizied housing project in Columbus, designed for family housing. With 40 two-story townhouse-styled three bedroom apartments, the project is arranged with five housing blocks and four pedestrian "mew" entries on a triangular site. Each townhouse has a fenced front yard, storage structure and entry gate facing one of the mews. The site is located in a predominantly working class residential area in east Columbus, bordered by a railroad and adjacent industrial area.

With wood-frame construction, the design found additional cost efficiency with back-to-back apartments and typically three common walls per unit to minimize the overall perimeter and exterior wall construction. The simple pitched asphalt shingle roofs and shed roof dormers provide clerestory natural lighting and ventilation into the apartments and a distinctive building profile. The living room opens directly onto the private front yards.

A separate community building, with a common day room, office and maintenance garage, features a large shed roof and large window. All of the buildings are horizontal cedar clapboard stained gray, with white window frames, doors and picket fences. An entry gate, seat walls and trash enclosures are constructed of concrete and painted white.

Parking is located adjacent to the railroad tracks and connects directly to the mews. Landscaping has been incorporated around the site perimeter and in the front yard to create an allée within the mews. The project includes a playground and a community plaza.

Architect's fees paid by
The Cummins Foundation
Architecture Program

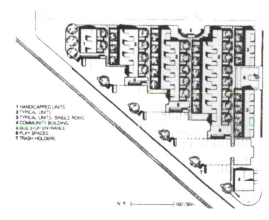

Site Plan

1987 Fire Station No. 5

1983 - 1987   100 Goeller Court

Susana Torre, *design architect*
Charles Budd, *project architect*
George Gianakopoulous, *partner*
Wank Adams Slavin Associates
New York, New York

Architect's comment:
"The garage is the major piece of the building, so you can't put it in the back, as in a house, and in this case the building doesn't have a back - sitting on a triangular lot, it's exposed on all sides... (My objective was) to extend the city's tradition of innovation in firefighting techniques and facilities to the new building, in terms of state-of-the-art equipment, as well as the internal layout, relationship to the site, energy conservation, and aesthetics."
Susana Torre, 1984

In Fire Station No. 5, the architect organized the plan into two overlapping squares – one for the fire apparatus, the other for people. The latter square is subdivided into a public wing (containing a metal-clad silo which houses stairs and a fireman's pole) and a residential wing. The second level includes bedrooms, each with three pull-down beds to serve individuals on the three different shifts. Each functional area in the public wing has its own exterior entrance, and all areas have quick and unobstructed access to the apparatus room.

Located west of Columbus on former farmland and adjacent to and serving a rapidly growing planned residential area, Fire Station No. 5 posed contrasting design issues for the architects. These issues were resolved by using understated references to familiar rural symbols of silos and barns. The idea of opposites continues in the use of materials: metals against brick, cold colors against warm, an exposed steel frame within a masonry envelope.

To preserve as much of the triangular plot as possible, including a small brook, the building is placed on one corner. The site is bordered on two sides by main roads. On the third side is a dead-end spur which was widened for parking and equipped with a basketball court.

Susana Torre was selected as the architect though an invited design competition process. She began her process with a study of the fire station as a building type.

Architect's fees paid by
The Cummins Foundation Architecture Program

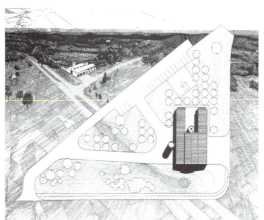

Site Plan / Aerial Perspective

1988 St. Peter's Lutheran Church

1980 - 1988   719 Fifth Street

Gunnar Birkerts
Birmingham, Michigan

Client's statement:
"As the spire of the church reaches towards heaven, so the souls of its members yearn for oneness with God."

Architect's statement:
"Getting light into buildings and getting ambience through daylight is part of my work that people recognize."
          Gunnar Birkerts

Lifting itself among the surrounding spires of First Christian Church, First Presbyterian Church and First United Methodist Church, the 186-foot copper-clad spire of St. Peter's Lutheran Church provides a magnificent addition to the skyline of downtown Columbus.

The building design incorporates the contrasting duality of orthogonal forms on the south and circular geometry to the north. The structure is reinforced concrete, clad in brick and copper. The conical roof, bell sphere and spire feature copper sheeting.

The unique interior seating for 1,000 is designed to seat the whole congregation on a single level, with the use of a balcony. The sanctuary expresses the exterior blend of flat and curved surfaces with white plaster surfaces. The north radiused wall is accented with narrow, deeply recessed windows in a pattern repeated throughout the sanctuary. The south is dominated by massive fin walls, with windows stretching from floor to ceiling to provide natural light. Artificial and natural lighting, maple furniture, limestone and maple liturgical furnishings provide a variety of interior textures. Two off-axis circles create an inner and outer sanctuary, drawing the congregation together. The well-defined space of the inner nave gives the visitor a feeling of being in a church within a church and provides a setting for smaller functions such as weddings.

Four features of the congregation's 1904 sanctuary are incorporated into the new building – the bell, the Holtkamp organ which was rebuilt in 1989 by Steiner-Reck, the oval marble altar top and the stained glass window of Christ in Gethsemane. School children paid for moving the window with their weekly chapel offerings.

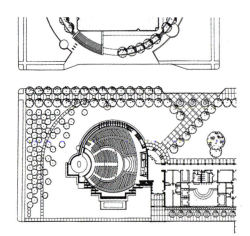

Site Plan

1989 Hope Elementary School

Highway 9, Hope, Indiana

John J. Casbarian
Danny M. Samuels
Robert H. Timme
Taft Architects
Houston, Texas

Architect's statement:
"The design ... organizes both interior and exterior public functions along a linear street. Evoking the London shopping arcades, the street is modulated by bay windows and pavilions which mark the intersection of separate wings. Playing fields and gardens are extensions of this system. Clad in red brick and white polished concrete block, the banded pattern provides a variety of scale references for all the children."
Taft Architects

This new elementary school on the outskirts of Hope replaced the original town school which at one time housed grades 1-12 in this northeastern Bartholomew County community. Trustees of the Flatrock-Hawcreek School Corporation applied to The Cummins Foundation for inclusion in the Architecture Program, and the request was granted.

The architects gathered ideas from students, teachers, board members and community residents to develop concepts for the building. Teachers' requests included ample storage space, large window openings, bulletin board space and restrooms in the kindergarten through third grade classrooms. People in the community asked for a building that would be functional, and economical to operate, with a specific desire not to have a flat roof. The regulation sized gymnasium was designed to seat the entire 500 student body for programs and convocations.

The center hallway is the "main street" of the building with large foyers at each end. It creates a mall-like appearance with classroom windows interspersed with masonry pillars. Carpeted classrooms are designed to have one wall of windows, one of storage and the remaining walls with tack board space. The two-level library is an octagonal room projecting from the center hall, with booths around the upper level for students to sit and peruse books.

The facility is located close to a park which utilizes the remainder of the 20 acre site. An old one-room school building has been moved to the site as a reminder of the Hope community's rural past.

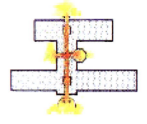

Architect's fees paid by
The Cummins Foundation
Architecture Program

1990 Bartholomew County Jail
543 Second Street

Don M. Hisaka
Don. M. Hisaka and Associates
Cambridge, Massachusetts

Architectural Consultant
Nolan Bingham
Columbus, Indiana

2008 Addition
RQAW Corp.
Indianapolis, Indiana

Built of brick and rough-faced limestone blocks, the Bartholomew County Jail design is compatible with nearby City Hall and the County Courthouse. The classical architectural design form and details enclose a technologically advanced building designed to be in compliance with modern, enlightened laws of criminal justice. The traditional building form creates a memorable civic image.

The oval-shaped design is the most dramatic element of the design, topped with a wire-mesh dome for outdoor recreation. The building has two distinct sections. A linear two-story front houses the law enforcement offices and public entry. The functional 16-sided irregular polygon contains the secure detention facility. These sections are connected by a bridging tower containing stairs and elevators.

The two-story public entry organizes different public and work areas, articulated with portals leading to ground floor offices and a monumental stair allowing access to an interior balcony, visitation areas for inmates and their relatives, and the offices of the sheriff and staff. The site is a city block outlined with honey locust trees, a continuation of the Second Street landscaping in front of City Hall and The Republic.

The rectangular jail addition utilized a precast concrete modular design, with inset thin-brick to match the original building.

Architect's fees paid by
The Cummins Foundation
Architecture Program

1990 Streetscape

1988 - 1990

Washington Street, 2nd to 8th Streets

Paul Kennon, *design principal*
Michael Shirley, *assistant design principal*
Caudill Rowlett Scott (CRS)
Houston, Texas

Landscape Architect
Michael Van Valkenburgh
Michael Van Valkenburgh and Associates
Cambridge, Massachusetts

Traffic and Parking Planning
Pflum, Klausmeier & Gehrum Associates
Indianapolis, Indiana office

Commons block streetscape
Carol Wolff, Sean Sanger
Copley Wolff Design Group
Boston, Massachusetts

2011 Revisions

Architect's fees paid by
The Cummins Foundation
Architecture Program 1990, 1993

Architect Paul Kennon was given the challenge to create an attractive, accessible, pedestrian-friendly downtown. Through a series of community-wide meetings and focus groups, the decision was made to return Washington Street to two-way traffic, improve the lighting and provide other urban amenities. Michael Shirley and Michael Van Valkenburgh completed the design after Paul's untimely death.

New street lights, complete with banners, provide increased illumination to sidewalks and storefronts. Two-way traffic along Washington Street eases traffic movement to retail establishments on both sides of the street. Removal of parking meters from the central business area, coupled with leased spaces for employees in adjacent parking lots, encourages downtown shopping. Concrete paver bricks create plazas at major intersections; brick sidewalks use contrasting colors for pattern; corner amenities include marble-topped benches, trash receptacles, and concrete planters with seasonal plantings, junipers and pear trees.

Funding for the Streetscape project was provided by city, county and state governments, Cummins Engine Foundation, local financial institutions, and the public through "Adopt-A-Brick." This program allowed people, organizations and businesses to contribute to Streetscape and have names or messages inscribed on bricks. Over 7,000 inscribed bricks have been laid in the Washington Street sidewalks.

The Washington Street sidewalk design in front of the new Commons and on 3rd Street were modified by Copley Wolff Design Group with strong diagonal bands that related to the skew of the new playground form. Sloped planters, custom bollards and additional named bricks were incorporated at the 3rd and Washington Street corner.

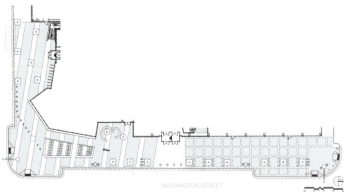

2011 Sidewalk Brick Paver Plan

1992 Columbus Regional Hospital

1988 - 1992 2400 East 17th Street Master Plan and Phase I Expansion

Robert A.M. Stern, *design principal*
Graham S. Wyatt, *partner-in-charge*
Robert A.M. Stern Architects
New York, New York

Associate Architects
The Falick / Klein Partnership

1996 Robert A.M. Stern Architects
Phase II Expansion New York, New York

Founded in 1917, Columbus Regional Hospital began as Bartholomew County Hospital, with its facilities growing haphazardly on a site now composed of 38 acres, bisected by Haw Creek. Robert Stern was hired to create a master plan utilizing the best of the existing buildings and new buildings to create the most advanced, cost-effective healthcare and services for the southeast Indiana region.

In contrast to the typical sterile hospital design, Stern's design was inspired by a more friendly hotel character and is specifically Midwestern in style, referencing Frank Lloyd Wright, as well as the Irwin House and First Christian Church.

Breaking down the scale of the campus buildings, two-story pavilions (one providing comprehensive cancer care and the other offering private birthing suites) with intervening courtyards are connected to the existing building by a double-height concourse. A new two-story entry lobby consolidates patient admitting, registration, and waiting areas. A glass-enclosed dining pavilion surrounded with a trellis provides a pleasant atmosphere for relatives and visitors.

Warm beige brick and green clay-tile roofs create an exterior in harmony with the neighborhood and Columbus' architectural heritage. Interior design, colors and furnishings emphasize comfort and convenience to minimize patient and family anxiety. Distinctive landscape plantings enhance the campus atmosphere.

The master plan included two medical office buildings on the west side of Haw Creek which has been bridged with a tree-lined boulevard to create a gateway entrance to the comprehensive parklike setting of the healthcare campus.

Architect's fees paid by
The Cummins Foundation
Architecture Program

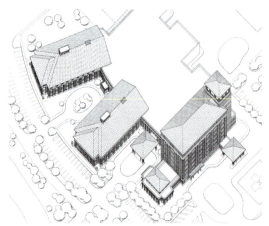
Axonometric Site Plan

1992 Mill Race Park

1989 - 1993
50 Fifth Street

Park design and Landscape Architect
Michael Van Valkenburgh
Michael Van Valkenburgh and Associates
Cambridge, Massachusetts

Architecture (structures)
Stanley Saitowitz
San Francisco, California

Client's statement:
A 50-member committee of volunteers was formed by Mayor Robert Steward in 1984 to oversee the community's 500th celebration of Christopher Columbus' journey to the New World. The park was officially dedicated in 1992, with construction completed the following year.

Architect's fees paid by
The Cummins Foundation
Architecture Program

Located in an oxbow bend of the Flatrock River on the western edge of downtown Columbus, this 85 acre site had previously been an industrial area and had informally evolved with recreational activities, despite frequent flooding. Mill Race Park is a testament to the collaborative spirit of design with the contributions of the community, the Park and Recreation department, architectural structures by Stanley Saitowitz and the overall park design concept by Michael Van Valkenburgh.

A round pond provides a central orientation feature which is experienced from a loop road that roughly follows the river edge. A historic covered bridge was relocated to the park. The mounded crescent shaped amphitheater at the park entry provides the other grand gesture in the park for public concerts and events. A landscaped parking lot is integrated into the park next to a remnant tannery foundation wall, bounded by a preexisting allée of linden trees. While much of the natural setting was preserved, hardy new species were selected that could withstand saturated soils and weather drought. The overall affordability and durability of the site materials reflects an intentional efficiency for both construction and low maintenance of the park. The park was constructed with the assistance of the Atterbury Job Corps.

A series of "follies" that become micro-destinations and serve specific functions are distributed throughout the park. Designed in collaboration with Stanley Saitowitz, these structures highlighted with red painted metal include an observation tower, a boathouse, a river lookout, a fishing pier, the amphitheater stage, an arbor, restrooms and picnic shelters. Note that the restroom's curved roof implies an "M" and "W". The 84-foot high observation tower provides a "bird's-eye view" of downtown Columbus.

Site Plan

1995 Breeden Realtors Office Building

700 Washington Street

Thomas H. Beeby
Gary M. Ainge
Hammond Beeby and Babka, Inc.
Chicago, Illinois

Breeden Inc. understood the value of Columbus' commitment to architectural design excellence, commissioning nationally recognized Thomas Beeby of Chicago to design a distinctive, yet still modest, office building for its headquarters. Located on the northern entry to downtown on Washington Street, the "main street" of Columbus, it created a prominent corner with its recessed glass rotunda entry. The corner brick plaza acts as a terminus to the downtown streetscape. It creates an important and harmonious "gateway" entrance from the north to downtown.

The size and shape of the building are consistent with the downtown character. The two-story building is arranged with two brick wings flanking a central glazed entry rotunda surmounted with a copper dome. The main entry incorporates full-height cast-aluminum columns with decorative capitals and bases, as well as a bronze logo in the terrazzo lobby floor. The mottled brick exterior walls are articulated with shaped limestone sills and capitals, as well as an aluminum curtain wall with Vermont green marble spandrel panels.

The "L"-shaped building plan was developed to allow primary access and street presence for the owner's offices in the two wings on the first floor level with leasable tenant space on the second floor accessible from an auxiliary lobby at the rear of the building. The building is slightly set back from both Washington and 7th Streets, allowing for street front landscaping and privacy.

The predominant architectural impression is a simple functional building, highlighted by abstract classical details.

1995 Columbus Area Visitors Center

Fifth and Franklin Streets — *former home of* John V. Storey

Addition & Renovation

Kevin Roche
Kevin Roche John Dinkeloo and Associates
Hamden, Connecticut

Associate Architect
Todd Williams
Todd Williams and Associates
Columbus, Indiana

Landscape Architect
Jack Curtis
Monroe, Connecticut

"Yellow Neon Chandelier" and "Persians"
Dale Chihuly, *glass sculptor*
Seattle, Washington

2011-2012 Interior Renovation

Jonathan Hess
Browning Day Mullins Dierdorf
Indianapolis, Indiana

The original 1864 Italianate house was the home of John V. Storey. With the formation of the Columbus Area Visitors Center in 1972, the house had been renovated by Bruce Adams for its new use. In 1995, Kevin Roche created a sensitive "matching" addition including a gift shop, display areas, restrooms, and a basement. A two story bay window with an open stairway behind denotes the old and the new. The "Yellow Neon Chandelier" and the "Persians" by Dale Chihuly glow within this naturally and artificially lit space.

The Visitors Center is the starting point for Columbus architectural tours, including the Miller House and Garden. Video presentations tell the story of Columbus' famous architecture and its value in creating a better community. The 2012 interior renovations, inspired by the interior design of Alexander Girard, provide a more expansive presentation and waiting room, featuring Herman Miller modern furniture.

The landscaping includes zelkova trees planted along Fifth Street and aristocrat pears on Franklin Street. Sugar tyme crabapples are located in the grass area to the rear of the building. The beds of bowles vinca ground cover located between the Visitors Center and the Library are planted with spring blossoming bulbs, with a multi-stem skyline honey locust.

Addition and renovation costs were supported by
Xenia S. Miller, Clementine Tangeman,
The Heritage Fund of Bartholomew County
and The Cummins Foundation.

1996 Cummins Columbus Engine Plant

1994 - 1996   500 Central Avenue (Haw Creek Boulevard)

1996 Addition & Renovations	**Kevin Roche** Kevin Roche John Dinkeloo and Associates Hamden, Connecticut
	Landscape Architect **Jack Curtis** Monroe, Connecticut
1960 & 1965 Additions & Renovations	**Harry Weese** Harry Weese and Associates Chicago, Illinois

Cummins main engine plant has been in the same location for over 70 years and has grown piecemeal to 1.3 million square feet. Kevin Roche was asked to renovate the existing plant, design an office addition and create a new entry on the east side facing Central Avenue.

The two-story glass office addition is composed of flush butt-jointed square glass and stainless steel panels, contrasting to the ribbed precast concrete panels in previous additions and renovations designed by Harry Weese. The white-patterned "fritted" glass consists of tiny dots, white on the outside to reflect heat and black on the inside to allow a "clear" view out. The glass appears opaque during the day, while revealing the office interiors at night.

The main entry features a large Cummins logo on a two story entry canopy, a glass wall and a sloped skylight over a drive-up large enough for semi-trucks. The double-height lobby behind the entry canopy is distinguished with clear glass exterior and interior windows that look into the reorganized plant assembly line, visually connecting the office workers and visitors to production.

The main Central Avenue entry is highlighted by a tree-lined boulevard with visitor parking, and landscaped parking for employees on both sides.

1997 Columbus "Gateway" projects

1986 - 1999   State Road 46

I-65 overpass and 2nd Street bridge design
Jean M. Muller
J. Muller International
Chicago, Illinois office

Master Planning, 1988
Paul Kennon, *design principal*
Caudill Rowlett Scott (CRS)
Houston, Texas

Landscape Design
Michael Van Valkenburgh
Michael Van Valkenburgh and Associates (MVVA)
Cambridge, Massachusetts

Golf Course design
Hurdzan Design Group
Columbus, Ohio

Concept Design 1991-1993
Robert Venturi, Steven Izenour
Venturi, Scott Brown & Associates (VSBA)
Philadelphia, Pennsylvania

Master Planning
Pflum, Klausmeier & Gehrum Associates (PKGA)
Indianapolis, Indiana office

Project Manager, Civil Engineering
Woolpert, Inc.
Indianapolis, Indiana

Pedestrian System, "People Trail", 1986-1996
Storrow Kinsella Associates (SKA)
Indianapolis, Indiana

In 1988, Paul Kennon led a community planning process to develop a landscaped "front door" to downtown Columbus along State Road 46 from interstate I-65 to the west. The concept was to demonstrate to federal and state agencies, as well as other communities, how small cities off the interstate system could identify themselves and attract the driver-by into their city. The design team of CRS, MVVA and Hurdzan Design Group initially proposed landscape and art at the Interstate 65 interchange, a planted corridor on State Road 46, bicycle and pedestrian trails, a golf course and a new bridge to downtown.

In 1991, VSBA in association with PKGA, MVVA, SKA and Woolpert elaborated on the idea with super graphics, landscaping and lighting. They proposed a "Welcome to Columbus" sign on a gateway truss spanning the highway and a series of custom designed multi-colored light fixtures rhythmically located in a central median.

1997 saw the first constructed gateway project by Jean Muller, a twin-arched overpass bridge at the I-65 intersection. The red arches emerge between the two interstate lanes, with rods supporting cantilevered beams below the concrete roadway. The unique signal-controlled diamond interchange below was a new concept in Indiana, less expensive than a conventional cloverleaf and requires significantly less right-of-way.

The 2nd Street bridge into downtown Columbus over the White River was completed in 1999. The bridge is fully suspended from center-locking quadripod pylons and two radiating rows of 40 cable stays. The rerouted west bound traffic of State Road 46 aligns an entry vista centered on the historic courthouse tower, with Eliel Saarinen's First Christian Church's modern bell tower seen in the distance.

Gateway proposal (Venturi, Scott Brown and Associates, Inc.)

1997 Veterans Memorial
Bartholomew County Veterans Memorial, Courthouse Square

Maryann Thompson
Charles Rose
Thompson and Rose Architects
Cambridge, Massachusetts

Landscape Architecture
Michael Van Valkenburgh
Michael Van Valkenburgh and Associates
Cambridge, Massachusetts

Associate Architect
Todd Williams
Todd Williams and Associates
Columbus, Indiana

A grid of 25 limestone pillars, each 40-feet high, serves as a memorial to Bartholomew County veterans of twentieth-century wars. With its rock-cut limestone exterior, the memorial appears as a monolithic block from a distance. The space within the pillars is intense, creating a haven of meditation. The architects were selected through an invited competition, their winning design included a request for the community to submit personal letters and journals written by veterans and their families.

Names of veterans, who gave their lives, as well as excepts from the requested letters and journals were engraved into the smooth face of the limestone interior. Visitors experience a layered passage into the heart of the field of pillars in which the recorded experience of the veterans becomes more and more intimate as one delves deeper into the space. The memorial places past occurrences and deeds within the contemporary culture of the county, and allows future generations to understand the histories of their families, county and country.

The memorial is tied to the land and to its locale: the grid of the pillars complements the grid of the city and the grid of flowering trees. It also recalls the rectilinear patterns of the surrounding agricultural landscape. The architects worked with materials quarried in Indiana.

Architect's fees paid by
The Cummins Foundation
Architecture Program

The memorial offers a profound and meditative space, a solemn experience which engenders a powerful sense of communal gratitude to those who have made the ultimate sacrifice. The upward visual movement of the tapered columns, silhouetted by the sky, evokes a sense of awe. At night, lights embedded at the base illuminating the interior create a dramatic play of light and shadow.

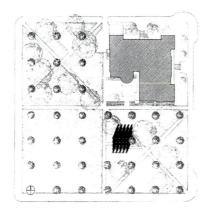

Courthouse Square Site Plan

BARTHOLOMEW COUNTY MEMORIAL FOR VETERANS

1997   The Republic Printing Center
3330 West International Court, Woodside Industrial Center

Peter F. Spittler
Celso R. Gilbert
Denver L. Brooker
Charles A. Rosati
GSI Architects, Inc. (Forum Architects)
Cleveland, Ohio

The printing and distribution facility was designed to house the print production capacity for several of the Brown family newspapers including The Republic (Columbus), the Daily Journal (Johnson County), and The Brown County Democrat (Nashville), as well as the expansion into commercial printing.

The new facility features a 160-foot transparent glass front visible to the interstate to showcase the upgraded technology of the pressroom, similar to the original design of The Republic by SOM. Accessibility and visibility were determining factors in selecting the 8.5 acre site adjacent to Interstate 65. The building design was influenced by the geometric simplicity of its architectural predecessor in downtown Columbus. It is laid out on a circular plan intersected by a strong horizontal axis to the north defining the pressroom and by the stepped, angular "bustles" of the mail room, with storage areas to the west. The sweep of the east façade, punctuated by a trellis canopied at the employee and visitor entrances, is counterbalanced by the linear pressroom that anchors the design.

The primary exterior materials are glass, metal panels and painted metal commonly associated with industry and technology, but rendered here with refined detailing and a palette which includes terracotta brown, referencing Indiana soil. The rooftop mechanical elements are arranged beneath an articulated yellow enclosure and clerestory windows illuminate the mailroom area.

1998 Fire Station No. 6

1900 W. County Road 450 S.

William Rawn
William Rawn and Associates
Boston, Massachusetts

Architect's statement:
"In a long line of famous Columbus fire stations, such as the Leighton Bowers designed Station No. 1 and the Venturi & Rauch designed Station No. 4, Fire Station No. 6 stands as a contemporary civic icon designed specifically for the fast-moving rural highway in the southern sector of Columbus."
William Rawn and Associates

Fire Station No. 6, located seven miles south of downtown, was built to protect the modern facilities of Woodside Industrial Park and the Cummins Midrange Engine Plant.

The bold but simple curved roof, essentially an asymmetrical "S" turned on its side, creates "fronts" for the traffic moving both directions on the parallel Highway 450, giving this public building its unique identity. East and west end walls are fabricated of glass blocks and a trio of overhead doors situated within a steel frame, giving it a crisp, contemporary feeling. In the daytime; the walls read as a black and white grid, at night the building becomes a beacon as it glows from within. The arch with cut out letters over the garage doors provides a centralized foil to the roof profile. The true front that faces the highway is clad in stone textured concrete masonry infilled in the steel structure, with a continuous four-foot high window.

The long one-story brick building houses the fire station office, as well as the exercise and residential quarters to provide privacy for the firefighters. It's alignment with the edge of the woods echoes the linearity of the highway. The building, with its flowing front, its long low brick form and glass elements was inspired by Kevin Roche's Cummins Midrange Engine Plant's luminous glass box located a half-mile west.

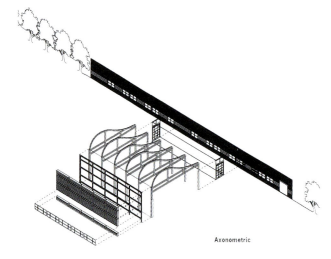
Axonometric

 Architect's fees paid by
The Cummins Foundation
Architecture Program

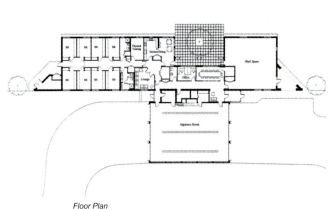
Floor Plan

1998   "Friendship Way" - Alley Walkway Projects
Washington Street, mid-block westside alley between Fourth and Fifth Streets

William Johnson
William J. Johnson Associates
Seattle, Washington

Associate Landscape Architects
Storrow Kinsella Associates
Indianapolis, Indiana

Neon Sculpture
Cork Marcheschi
San Francisco, California

The pedestrian alleyway improvement program included the extension of the 1990 Streetscape project by means of a similar rhythmic sidewalk brick paving pattern, landscaping and distinctive lighting. English ivy, as an evergreen ground cover, is the predominate plant material. Trellises in the middle and at the end of the alley carry flowering clematis and honeysuckle vines. Flowering perennials are planted at the bases of the trellises.

The bricks that form the alleyway located between Fourth and Fifth Streets (400 block) were a gift from the citizens of Miyoshi, Columbus' sister city in Japan, who contributed more than $35,000 through their purchase of named paving bricks for the project. Called "Friendship Way", the south wall of the alleyway features an animated neon sculpture that "moves" light and changes colors in circles, squares and lengthy tubes. A wood bench provides a resting spot at the Washington Street alley entrance.

A 1994 alley project is located between Sixth and Seventh Streets (600 block), connecting Washington Street and the Franklin Street parking lot, funded by SIECO Inc. and Kirr Marbach & Company, whose properties are adjacent to the alley. A curvilinear, flowing arc is achieved by carving lenses of plant material out of the paving field in stepped increments.

North of Home Federal Bank, a walkway between Fifth and Sixth Streets (500 block) features a granite topped bench, goose-neck light poles and the recommended landscaping.

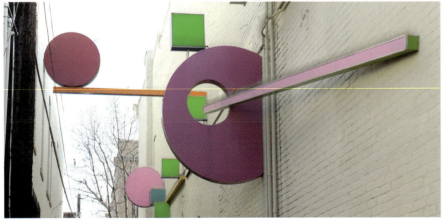

Neon Sculpture

Friendship Alley, 400 block - westside

500 block - eastside

600 block - eastside

1998 Hope Library

1994 - 1998   638 Main Street, Hope, Indiana

Deborah Berke
Deborah Berke Partners
New York, New York

Associate Architects
Veszey Parrot & Shoulders
Evansville, Indiana

Architect's statement:
"In a place that describes itself as "a surprising little town" the library is, in a sense, the architectural glue that binds the community."
    Deborah Berke

Located on the east side of the downtown square of Hope, Indiana, about fifteen miles northwest of Columbus, this 6,000 square foot, fully computerized branch of the Bartholomew County Public Library serves this community as a civic center. This modest brick library, with the adjacent branch bank designed by Harry Weese, is an unexpected infusion of modern architecture into this traditional townscape.

The building's low height, iron-spotted bricks, steel windows and metal awnings relate to the neighboring branch bank and the commercial structures. A zinc clad monitor rises above the brick wall to create a distinctive profile, expressing a grand space within. The zinc panels have darkened and developed a soft patina over time. The simple indentation of brickwork above the windows provides simple architectural detailing. Look for the word "HOPE" on the north ramp retaining wall.

Although extremely simple in plan and contextual architectural language, the library plays an important civic role beyond its strict programmatic function. It serves as an after-school gathering center and is designed to be particularly child-friendly. It is also frequented by elderly residents at all times of the day. The reading room's asymmetrical sweeping ceiling rises to a light monitor above large northern facing windows to provide natural lighting for comfortable daytime reading, and creates a grand civic place. The interior is finished in maple paneling and Indiana limestone. The Douglas fir ceiling is supported on arched laminated timber beams. Large steel windows allow daylight into the library and emit light at night, causing the building to glow.

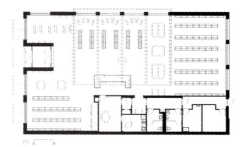
Floor Plan

Architect's fees paid by
The Cummins Foundation
Architecture Program

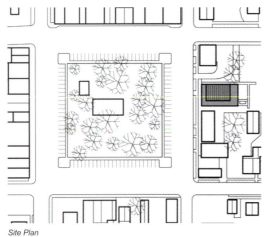
Site Plan

2001 Cummins Child Development Center

1997 - 2004   650 Pleasant Grove

Including
2004 Addition

Carlos Jimenez
Carlos Jimenez & Associates
Houston, Texas

Associate Architects
CSO Architects
Indianapolis, Indiana

Landscape Architect
Jack Curtis
Monroe, Connecticut

Architect's statement:
"A miniature city for kids."
                Carlos Jimenez, 2001

The Child Development Center provides on-site child care services for up to 228 children for employees of Cummins working over two shifts. The one-level building occupies a corner site in a modest residential area next to the beautifully landscaped Central Avenue, Haw Creek and the adjacent Cummins manufacturing and research campus.

The simple industrially clad metal siding and brick building consists of interconnecting classrooms serving infants to toddlers, two-year olds to pre-schoolers. The building entry is pronounced with a projecting metal canopy and blue metal panels, with an adjacent meeting room highlighted with playful circular windows. The conference room and lobby area are daylighted with clerestory dormers. A continuous single-loaded corridor, with large windows at the lobby for the adults and low windows for children, wraps around a central playground area. The structure's simple shed roof slopes down from the high exterior walls shielding the internal activities from the street to a lower scale at the courtyard, collecting natural light.

Each of the classrooms is visible to the corridor with large windows, allowing parents to watch their children from outside the room without disturbing the activities within. A special room is also designated as a storm shelter with protective rolling grilles and a concrete roof. The 2004 addition added four classrooms and another outdoor play area.

The facility was closed in 2008 due to the historic Haw Creek flood and reopened in 2010 after substantial remediation to the interiors.

Floor Plan

2001 West Hill Plaza Branch Bank

4190 Jonathan Moore Pike

First Financial Bank (*originally* Irwin Union Bank)

Carlos Jimenez
Carlos Jimenez & Associates
Houston, Texas

Associate Architect
Todd Williams
Todd Williams and Associates
Columbus, Indiana

This branch bank was a prototype design intent on maximizing spatial flexibility, site and technological adaptability for the branch banks, completed in Columbus and Seymour, Indiana.

The simple square plan has a central vaulted space where flexible and open offices are located. It is also a banking hall, a lobby, and an open container receiving light from both ends of its continuous sectional arc. All other bank functions such as tellers, vaults, restrooms, private offices, mechanical and storage, wrap around the central space. The layout can be rotated to accommodate different site conditions, just as the drive-through teller's canopy can be hinged from another wall.

The design aims to balance two types of banking: the personal one-to-one relationship between banker and customer, and the more expedient transactions offered by drive-through tellers. Two distinct roof forms highlight this difference while asserting their interdependence. The exterior materials are brick, clear anodized aluminium and clear glass. The entry is projected with horizontal metal ribbed siding and full glass doors.

2002 St. Paul's Episcopal Church
2651 California Street

Addition/Renovation

Thomas Beeby
Hammond, Beeby, Babka (HBB)
Chicago, Illinois

The original St. Paul's Episcopal Church building was designed in 1959 and in the mid-1990's church leaders realized that they had outgrown their existing facilities. St. Paul's engaged HBB to assess their existing facilities and determine their needs for future growth.

The new classroom addition is sympathetic in design to the original building. Its proportions and massing were designed so that the "A"-framed sanctuary remained the predominant element. HBB emphasized continuity rather than juxtaposition of new against old to unify the building composition to meet the desires of the congregation. The unifying feature is a simple exterior colonnade, that also acts as a loggia, visually connecting the classrooms to the sanctuary and defining a courtyard space which includes a memorial garden.

2002 St. Bartholomew Catholic Church

1999 - 2002   1306 27th Street / Home Ave.

Steven R. Risting, *design principal*
William Browne, Jr., *managing principal*
Ratio Architects
Indianapolis, Indiana

Stained Glass
Elizabeth Devereaux, *artist*
Chico, California

Landscape
Dean Shertz
Columbus, Indiana

Architect's statement:
"The nautilus shape of the worship space was inspired by the parishes' desire to relate to nature and a fan-shaped seating plan that keeps the parish close to the central altar. The bell tower is the main structural support for the roof and the spiritual support for the church with the chapel containing the tabernacle at its base."
Steven Risting, 2002

St. Bartholomew Roman Catholic Church is the consolidation of two parishes into one. To complete the unification, they needed a single worship space for over 900 parishioners, as well as a large narthex for gathering, meeting rooms, a nursery and parish offices. They decided to build a new worship space, additional educational spaces and a new gymnasium on the site of their school.

The design evolved from a design competition, which began with the parish's request to create a design appropriate for a "traditional" parish in a "modern" community. The design investigated the architectural and material expression of Catholicism and the Vatican II referendum, the idea of procession from the secular to the sacred, and how to blend the new structure with the adjacent school.

The unique roof shape from the nautilus plan creates a large uplifting space above the large quarter circle, spiraling down to create a more intimate seating area. Two large north and east facing clerestory windows result, providing natural lighting and featuring an abstract stained glass window. The square shaped narthex engages the nautilus sanctuary, representing the relationship of man and nature. A large triangular clerestory skylight identifies the main entry above the nautilus shaped baptistry. The "perfect" shapes and regulating lines of the golden section and square are used throughout the building.

Primary building materials are golden buff Kasota limestone with three finish textures (rough cut, honed and polished) and diamond shaped copper shingles. The site is landscaped on the north with large natural stones tiered to allow natural light into the basement level. An addition to the school including a gymnasium, administrative offices and a new entry was also completed.

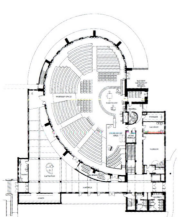

Floor Plan

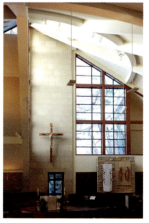

2005 Columbus Learning Center

1999 - 2005

4555 Central Avenue

Kevin Kennon
Kohn Peterson Fox
New York, New York

Associate Architects
Ratio Architects
Indianapolis, Indiana

Architect's statement:
"Columbus has left an indelible impression on my life and I am proud to be a part of its legacy."
Kevin Kennon, 1999

The Columbus Learning Center (CLC) is a state-of-the-art educational building developed to meet the demands of the community's educational and work force needs. The classrooms, laboratories, library and lecture hall are shared with over 7,000 students of Indiana University Purdue University Columbus (IUPUC), Purdue University School of Technology and Ivy Tech Community College.

The new building was located between the IUPUC/Purdue building and Ivy Tech, symbolically bridging the two entities, but remaining physically distinct. The primary two-story classroom building plan is arched, with a "floating" brick facade to the public front and a glass curtain wall with a two-story "Main Street" gallery space with a ramp on the landscape side. The double height library is contained in a separate brick and glass pavilion, that defines the northern edge of a central courtyard. A sloped roof lecture hall and student commons/dining anchors the other end of the building, connected with a skylit brick rotunda, just south of the building's main entry. The public front entry is defined with brick walls that reach out like open arms forming an outdoor room to welcome students and the community.

The building is managed by the Community Education Coalition (CEC), a partnership of education, business and community stakeholders focused on aligning and integrating community based educational programs with economic development and improvements to the quality of life in Columbus. The Center for Teaching and Learning, established by the CEC and based in the building, provides resources and support to teachers in the community from pre-school through college level, as well as adult continuing education programs.

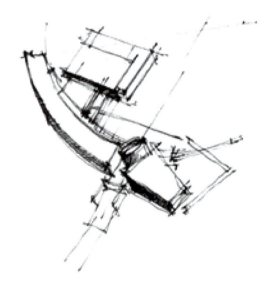

Design Architect's fees paid by
The Cummins Foundation Architecture Program

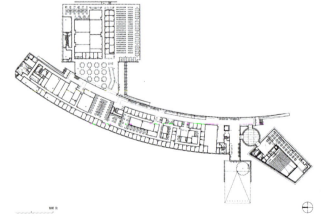

Floor Plan

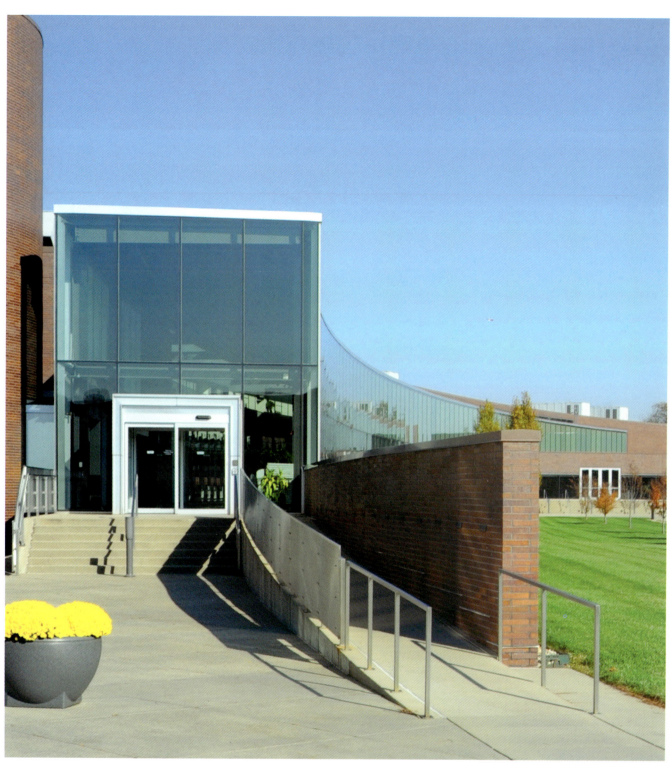

2006 Creekview Branch Bank

2004 - 2006
Creekview Plaza   First Financial Bank (*originally* Irwin Union Bank)

Deborah Berke
Deborah Berke Partners
New York, New York

Associate Architect
Todd Williams
Todd Williams and Associates
Columbus, Indiana

Owner's statement:
"...aspiration to improve the neighborhood by designing to a higher quality than the surrounding buildings without blowing the budget."
    Will Miller, CEO & President of Irwin Financial Corp., 2007

The branch bank is located on a site surrounded by the wide-open expanse of a strip shopping mall including two large "big-box" retail buildings, a car wash, a multiplex theater, chain restaurants and the inevitable sea of asphalt parking lots. A strategy was sought that would prevent the building, despite its modest size, from getting lost in this jumbled expanse. A bold and simple design gesture was developed.

The major component of the branch bank building is the drive-through banking, which the design acknowledges as an equal partner to more traditional walk-in banking rather than treating it as an afterthought. Floating above the masonry building, a "light box" spans both the drive-through lanes and the main banking hall inside. This translucent box, made of planks of structural channel glass, permits natural light to filter down into the banking hall. Owing to the mysterious, translucent quality of this glass, the 'Light Box' also glows outwardly as an ambiguous sculptural object that is neither building nor sign. It floats in the air, lending the new bank building a steady, quietly elegant presence that serves as a refreshing counterpoint to the heavy, sprawling 'big box' retail buildings nearby.

The orthogonal regularity of the bank's interior provides relief from the building's disorderly context. Oval light fixtures seem to float in the space, reinforcing the quality of airiness created by the "light box".

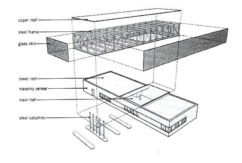

Floor Plan

2007 Central Middle School

2000 - 2007   725 7th Street

Ralph Johnson
Perkins + Will
Chicago, Illinois

Associate Architects
CSO Architects
Indianapolis, IN

Owner's statement:
"(The architects) guided us through a very thorough process that brought the community together in the spirit of true collaboration. The design is a clear reflection of our educational needs for the 21st Century."
    Mindy M. Lewis, BCSC board member
    and President, 2006

Central Middle School is a replacement for a 100-year old traditional school building, located in the architecturally significant downtown district and next to Lincoln Elementary School. The new building was organized on a new middle school educational model to serve 900 students in grades 7 and 8.

The building is zoned into two components, a public and an academic zone. The public zone in organized around a two-story Commons which acts as a multi-functional cultural hub and also serves as a cafeteria. This zone includes two gymnasiums, the media center, music rooms, a black box theater and the administrative offices. The academic zone is organized with groupings of classrooms angled off a spine of specialized science classrooms. Subdividing the school into team areas also breaks down the scale of the building, creating a supportive environment for the middle school team methodology.

The football field and track are located at the front of the school, on the site of the former school building. The building front is composed of a glass entry and media center framed above, as well as a brick wall with uniquely patterned window openings which creates a distinctive urban edge.

This was the architect's second design which was revised for cost savings, after the first design was defeated in a community referendum that included additions to several other schools and a new elementary school that were not constructed.

First Floor Plan

 Design Architect's fees paid by
The Cummins Foundation
Architecture Program

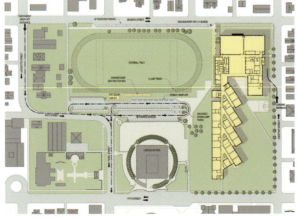

Site Plan

2009 Jackson Street Garage

2007 - 2009   401 Jackson Street - between 4th and 5th Streets

Fred Koetter
Susie Kim
Koetter Kim & Associates
Boston, Massachusetts

Associate Architect
Todd Williams
Todd Williams and Associates
Columbus, Indiana

The 400-car, four-level parking garage was the first structure built as a part of the 4th Street "Entertainment District" downtown redevelopment master plan by Koetter Kim & Associates, which included the redesign of the original Commons and Commons Mall.

While meeting the increased downtown parking needs, it was important that the parking garage provide an image and scale that supports the intended pedestrian and retail environment, as well as relate positively and graciously to Columbus' historic downtown buildings and street patterns. The three-story brick facade on 4th and 5th Streets reflects the contextual scale of the adjacent buildings with a modern grid. The 4th Street frontage includes space for retail or restaurants, which have successfully been occupied by two restaurants with outdoor sidewalk seating activating downtown street life.

The upper levels of the brick grid are detailed with a layering of metal grid and perforated metal siding to give a hint that this is a parking garage. The Jackson Street frontage, with the auto entry in the center of the block, reveals itself as a parking facility with its exposed concrete structure and decorative metal screens. The rhythm of the exposed structure relates to the arcade rhythm of the Post Office across the street and the Cummins Corporate Office Building. The garage lighting was carefully considered to let the structure glow in the evening. The 4th and Jackson Street corner glass stair and elevator tower is an open and inviting pedestrian entry.

The site was originally a landscaped parking lot, designed by Michael Van Valkenburgh, part of the 1998 Walkway Project.

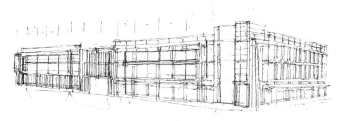

Architect's fees paid by
The Cummins Foundation Architecture Program

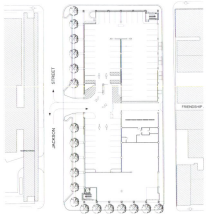

Floor Plan

2009 Commons Office Building

2007 - 2013   301 Jackson Street

Fred Koetter
Susie Kim
Koetter Kim & Associates
Boston, Massachusetts

Executive Architect & Collaborating Designer
Steven R. Risting
CSO Architects
Indianapolis, Indiana

2013 Addition

Addition Architect
Steven R. Risting
CSO Architects

Consulting Architect
Fred Koetter
Koetter Kim & Associates

Interior Design
Axis Architects
Indianapolis, Indiana

Original design fees supported by
Irwin-Sweeney-Miller Foundation

The four-story building was designed as a general office building for Cummins, who requested open offices and lots of natural lighting. Located on the site of the original Commons Mall, this was the second building constructed as a part of the downtown redevelopment master plan. Its primary glass curtain wall facade faces south toward the open Courthouse Square, allowing natural daylighting and spectacular views.

The main building entry on the corner of 3rd Street and the new Jackson Street, is emphasized with a projecting bay window above a projecting entry vestibule, recalling the historic bay windows of downtown and the modern detailing of the Irwin Union Bank. The top floor is recessed with expressed thin columns and a projecting cornice. The clear floor to ceiling glass is meticulously detailed with projecting horizontal mullions, sunscreens and end fins. The side walls are simplified with horizontal windows, patterned with offsetting translucent windows and vertical sun fins on the west facade. The lobby is understated with stone flooring, bamboo walls and a floating ceiling. The building is energy efficient and sustainable, achieving LEED Silver rating.

The five-story addition doubles the office area, with a four-story terraced atrium next to the existing building, providing daylight and social gathering spaces in the center of the expanded office floor. The connection between the new addition and the existing building features a "bow tie" project, for viewing up and down the street, and a "butterfly" inverted roof to direct daylight down into the interiors. The 4th Street front is reduced to three stories, to match the height of the adjacent Commons, with restaurants on the street level. The fourth floor features a corner terrace and a vegetated green roof.

Floor Plan

2009 Third Street Garage & The Cole

2008 - 2009

2nd and 3rd Street, between Brown and Jackson Streets

2013 apartments

Steven R. Risting
CSO Architects
Indianapolis, Indiana

The development of a downtown block for housing and parking was a part of the redevelopment strategic master plan to bring entertainment, work, education and housing to enliven the downtown. The prominent site serves as the west face of the Courthouse Square and creates gateway corners for those entering downtown from State Road 46 and its iconic entry bridge. Located between 2nd and 3rd Streets, Brown and Jackson Streets, it was originally a parking lot for the Commons Mall, whose two blocks were redeveloped with the new Commons, the Commons Office Building for Cummins, and new retail frontage on the reinstated Jackson Street.

Completed on 2009, the 700-car, five-level parking garage was constructed to serve the new Commons Office Building, and provide public parking and spaces for the apartment residents. The parking structure is located in the center of the block to allow the housing to wrap around it on three sides. While the main garage entry is on the south 2nd Street side for traffic flow reasons, driving under the housing project, the facade on 3rd Street features the public auto and pedestrian entries defined with the stair/elevator tower. The 3rd Street facade features street level brick columns, a perforated metal screen and an upper level architectural colonnade.

The Cole, the four-story housing project provides 146 one- and two-bedroom apartments. The primary east Courthouse Square facade features projecting bay windows and a cornice recalling the Washington Street Victorian buildings, with a couple of recesses to break up the scale of the building. The Jackson Street first floor frontage will provide additional downtown retail/restaurant space, as well as housing amenities. The west Brown Street side will include first floor walk-up apartments.

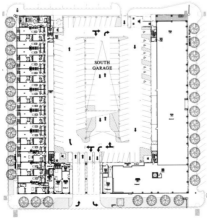

Site/Floor Plan

2011 Mill Race Center

2007 - 2011   148 Lindsey Street

William Rawn
Douglas Johnston, *design principal*
William Rawn and Associates
Boston, Massachusetts

Associate Architects
Ratio Architects
Indianapolis, Indiana

Transportation Center Architect
William Burd
Columbus, Indiana

Mill Race Center is a community center for active adults located in Mill Race Park. The facility's purpose is to develop a nationally recognized model for dynamic, comprehensive, collaborative programming for the age 50 plus population.

The gently curving blended brick building is sited to create superb views of the natural surroundings of Mill Race Park and maximize daylighting. The bricks were specially made four inches longer than normal bricks to emphasize the horizontality of the building. A double height dividable community/multipurpose room is clad with zinc siding and a projecting roof to shade the clerestory windows. The entry lobby is also double height, lit with clerestory windows, which progress to an exquisite glass enclosed lounge featuring a fireplace and wooden sun shade louvers. The facility includes a state-of-the-art fitness and rehabilitation center, classrooms, an art room, a woodworking shop and a computer lab.

Senior Services of Bartholomew County partnered with a variety of other organizations to develop this facility and share operational costs. Facility partners include the City of Columbus, Columbus Regional Hospital, IUPUC, Ivy Tech Community College, Elwood Staffing, Aging and Community Services and Just Friends Adult Day Care Services.

The site was able to be developed due to the relocation and the reconfiguration of the intersection of Indianapolis Road, Lindsey and 10th Street into a round-about. Leveraging federal funds also allowed for the construction of a transit center for the city bus system, as well as possible future intercity transportation services.

Design Architect's fees paid by
The Cummins Foundation
Architecture Program

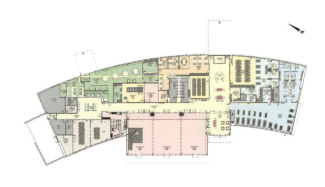

Floor Plan

2011 Advanced Manufacturing Center

2007 - 2011 4444 Kelly Street

Cesar Pelli
Darin C. Cook, *senior design associate*
Pelli Clarke Pelli
New Haven, Connecticut

Associate Architects
Ratio Architects
Indianapolis, Indiana

Architect's statement:
"This is a building whose purpose is extraordinary. This is a building that will contribute a great deal to Columbus today and many generations. A building that will be training youngsters....to allow them to pursue rich, fulfilling and productive lives."
     Cesar Pelli, 2009

Public statement:
"Common challenges and opportunities exist within regional companies in the manufacturing sector, providing an opportunity for the Center of Excellence to partner with academic centers to position this region as a magnet that would attract highly qualified experts and new companies."
     Report by the Columbus Economic
     Development Board, 1996

Officially named the Advanced Manufacturing Center of Excellence (AMCE), it is an education and workforce training center serving students and industry in Southeastern Indiana. The facility is designed for a science, technology, engineering, and math (STEM) curriculum, providing certification and degree programs, as well as development services for manufacturers.

The building contains integrated technology labs, classrooms, faculty offices, conference rooms and student/faculty common areas. With two central outdoor courtyards, the interior is filled with natural light with large perimeter and courtyard windows. The glass is fritted to control heat gain and glare. The building's simple steel structure is expressed with the perimeter columns and the roof framing exposed at the overhangs. The silver metal panel exterior and interior walls are non-load bearing to allow for flexibility for future needs or technology changes.

The AMCE building is located on the academic campus which includes buildings for Indiana University - Purdue University at Columbus (IUPUC), Ivy Tech Community College, Harrison College and the Columbus Learning Center.

AMCE was funded with grants from the Heritage Fund of Bartholomew County and the Lilly Endowment. Its programs are coordinated by the Community Education Coalition.

Design Architect's fees paid by
The Cummins Foundation
Architecture Program

Floor Plan

2011 The Commons

2007 - 2011

300 Washington Street

Fred Koetter
Susie Kim
Koetter Kim and Associates
Boston, Massachusetts

Executive Architects and Interior Design
Steven R. Risting
CSO Architects
Indianapolis, Indiana

Playground and streetscape design
Carol Wolff, Sean Sanger
Copley Wolff Design Group
Boston, Massachusetts

Public statements:
"No other building in Columbus better represents the spirit of this community. The Commons has been at the center of our community's life for more than 35 years. No other development in the downtown, or Columbus for that matter, will be as important a contributor to our economic growth and development as the new Commons. Its design says a lot about who we are, what we stand for and our belief in the future."
Tom Vujovich

"I think the new Commons is a great thing for the community, in large part because it has all of the old elements of The Commons that have meant so much to us, but those elements have all been enhanced."
Will Miller

Design & Construction supported by
public funds, private donors,
Irwin-Sweeney-Miller Foundation,
Heritage Fund of Bartholomew County, and
The Cummins Foundation Architecture Program

The original Commons designed by Cesar Pelli was a grand indoor public room, "an American piazza"; it was an anchor to a downtown shopping mall which revitalized the downtown in 1973. Unfortunately rising operating costs and substantial renovation cost estimates led to the decision to demolish and rebuild this important community center. The new Commons became the centerpiece of the new downtown master plan to revitalize downtown with improved public meeting and performance areas, street front retail, an enlarged indoor playground and the refurbished "Chaos I" sculpture by Jean Tinguely.

The new Commons features ultra-clear insulated glass, with a variety of fritting patterns, to showcase the new indoor public activities within and provide greater energy efficiency. The multi-purpose performance hall is raised to a new second floor under the original building's structure, featuring a stage with theatrical lighting and rigging. The zigzag windows are acoustical as well as architectural, framing views up and down the street. Escalators and stairs wrap around the "Chaos I" sculpture to maintain the indoor civic room and draw people to the second floor activities. Restaurants occupy the street front space below.

The corner glass playground pavilion is skewed and sloped to retain a view of the corner Courthouse tower and create a playful structure to house the new custom playground featuring the Luckey Climber, an interactive sculpture. A vegetated green roof on the new structure contributes to making this a sustainable project, targeting LEED silver rating.

The Commons Mall, occupying two downtown blocks, was extensively demolished in 2009, with the exception of Sears on Brown Street which retains the original reddish-brown tinted glass.

Floor Plan

Photo by Yukio Futagawa, GA 1981

3 lower photos by Susan Fleck

2012 Cummins Garage & Urban Elements

2011 - 2012

600 Jackson Street

Executive Architects/Engineers
StructurePoint
Indianapolis, Indiana

National Design Consultant
Kevin Roche
Kevin Roche John Dinkeloo and Associates
Hamden, Connecticut

Local Design Architect
Todd Williams
Todd Williams and Associates
Columbus, Indiana

2012 - 2014   **Urban Elements apartments**
600 Washington Street

Steven R. Risting
CSO Architects
Indianapolis, Indiana

With Cummins general office expansion into the Commons Office Building, Irwin Union Bank Office Building and 301 Washington Street, projecting over 3,000 downtown employees, there was a need for additional parking. Located between 6th and 7th Streets on a former parking lot, the five-level, 4-bay parking garage provides 954 parking spaces.

Constructed as an exposed concrete structure for cost efficiency, the design was selected through a design-build process. It features two glass stair towers on opposite corners, with an elevator on the Jackson Street corner. Since it was located across the street from Cummins corporate headquarters, Kevin Roche was involved as an architectural advisor, adding a matching concrete trellis, metal screens and vegetated "green" walls on the north and south sides. The parking garage was set back over 60 feet from the Washington Street front to allow for the development of more downtown housing.

Cummins selected a local developer to construct, own and operate the apartment project. Called Urban Elements, the design was influenced by apartments in New York, Chicago and Seattle, with the intention of creating luxury apartments for the internationally recruited professionals working downtown. The design features two-story loft style units, floor-to-ceiling windows, balconies and a roof-top terrace. The building profile steps back and the facade is articulated to break down the Washington Street frontage into smaller components. The limited amount of brick responds to the brick corners of the garage and the historic downtown buildings, while the extensive use of glass references Columbus' modern architecture on Washington Street. The ground floor includes retail and commercial activities.

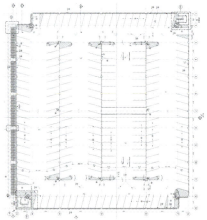

Apartments are a private development

Floor Plan

The **Columbus Arts District** has earned official state designation as an Indiana Cultural District, recognizing the significance of the city's rich collection of arts, architecture, entertainment and cultural offerings, and its vision for the future. The designation, announced Friday, December 7, 2012, by the Indiana Arts Commission, makes the Columbus Arts District one of only five official Indiana Cultural Districts in the state.

Mayor Kristen Brown's larger vision is to expand arts and cultural offerings across the Columbus community and provide opportunities for every adult and child in Columbus to participate in a wide-ranging variety of accessible art, culture and entertainment.

"We are deeply honored to receive this designation from the Indiana Arts Commission. This recognition serves as great validation of our tremendous collection of cultural assets we have today, and of our long-term vision to be the cultural and creative capital of the Midwest."
　　　　　Mayor Kristen Brown, 2012

Public Art in Columbus, Indiana

World-class public art complements the collection of modern architecture. Many of the initial masterpieces were recommended by the architects to create a focal point or public interaction within their buildings or in the outdoor space they created.

I.M. Pei suggested a sculpture for the library plaza that would act as a focal point and a "conductor" leading to the varying forms of Modern and Victorian architecture surrounding it. He wanted a sculpture that the public could interact with and touch. Pei recommended **Henry Moore**.

Cesar Pelli, the architect of the original Commons and Commons Mall, recommended a major work of art for the grand indoor space, stating. "We would like a great magnet, a focal point such as the old town clock... a place for people to meet and greet one another." Pelli recommended **Jean Tinguely**. When designing the playground for the new Commons, Carol Wolff of Copley Wolff Design Group, the playground designer, recommended an interactive custom built climber by architect and artist **Tom Luckey**.

Whether the art was recommended by the architect or later installed by the owner, world-class art has been incorporated in many of the public and private buildings including City Hall, schools, parks and Cummins. Among the most notable are the glass sculptures by **Dale Chihuly** at the Columbus Area Visitors Center and the Columbus Learning Center. Some of the sculptures have been created by local participation including the "Exploded Engine" assembled by Cummins employees and the sculpture at Hamilton Center designed and built by high school students.

The Columbus Area Arts Council organized a Public Sculpture Invitational in 2006 that resulted in the installation of large-scale works by nationally-known artists over several years. While the pieces were secured as temporary loans, many are still on display and two works were purchased to become a part of the City's permanent collection.

Irwin Garden

608 Fifth Street

Fountain sculptures

Boy with Duck
Sculptor unknown
After 1930

1932 **Elephant**
Golden Foundry
1932

Boy on a Dolphin
Sculptor unknown
After 1930

While a private garden, it is occasionally open to the public. Within the garden are distinctive sculptures incorporated into the gardens or fountains.

1971 Large Arch
Library Plaza, 536 Fifth Street

Henry Moore, *sculptor*
Much Hadham, Hertfordshire, England

Henry Moore may be the most influential public scupltor of the twentieth century, and his "Large Arch" is the largest of its kind in the nation. I.M Pei, the architect for the library, insisted that the plaza in front required a major sculpture to enliven and "hold the space", and he recommended Moore.

"Large Arch" reflects primitive simplicity and the power evident in monolithic sculpture of the past. Its abstract and organic form provide a contrast to the geometric shapes of the buildings surrounding it. I.M. Pei wanted the piece be interactive and requested that it be big enough for a couple to stroll through. Moore agreed on the condition that the opening would not be large enough for a car to drive through. Henry Moore said, "As a young sculptor I saw Stonehenge and ever since I've wanted to do work that could be walked through and around."

The sculpture is 20 feet tall, 12 feet wide and weighs five and one-half tons. It was designed at Moore's home and studio in England, and sandcast in bronze in fifty sections at the Herman Noack foundry in West Germany. The pieces, one-fourth to one-half inch thick, were welded with invisible seams. The green patina is a natural aged look for bronze, and was created through a special process, directed personally by the sculptor at the foundry. Henry Moore was 73 when he created "Large Arch".

The sculpture is a larger version of a smaller arch cast for the Sculpture Court at the Museum of Modern Art in New York City. The sculpture was commissioned by J. Irwin and Xenia S. Miller as a gift to the City of Columbus. "Large Arch" was dedicated with the library building on May 16, 1971.

1974 Chaos I
The Commons, 300 Washington Street

Jean Tinguely, *sculptor*
Zurich, Switzerland

2011 Restoration under the direction of
David Doup of Taylor Bros. Construction and
Robert McCoy of the Indianapolis Museum of Art

It seems fitting that the centerpiece of Columbus, Indiana, a city known for both its renowned architectural designs and its world-class manufacturing operation, would have a sculpture that successfully marries art and engineering.

"Chaos I" is a kinetic (moving) sculpture that cycles through a series of motions to simulate a day in the life. Cesar Pelli, the original Commons architect, recommended Jean Tinguely, wanting a focal point in the public indoor space that would make noise, be a clock, be a toy, be an interesting place to meet and be art. Tinguely was well known for his motion sculptures. Like much of his work, it is fabricated from scrap metal. Most of the materials for its construction were purchased locally, and the sculpture was built with the aid of local craftsmen working under the sculptor's direction. The sculpture is approximately 30 feet high and weighs almost seven tons. It is the largest Tinguely sculpture in the United States.

Jean Tinguely grew up in Basel, Switzerland, moved to France to pursue an art career doing both painting and sculpture. He belonged to the Parisian avant-garde in the mid-twentieth century. The sculptor considered "Chaos I" to be one of his best works, representing one of his most important ideas about art: "Life is movement. Everything transforms itself, everything modifies itself ceaselessly, and to try to stop it...seems to me a mockery of the intensity of life." The sculpture was commissioned by J. Irwin and Xenia S. Miller as a gift to the City of Columbus.

Sculptor's statement:
"I'll try to bring a problem to Columbus... It is my way to make a commentary about the problem of our civilization in one part. And in the other part I'm going to do a sculpture and a machine at the same time that will be new to me. I never did it before and I will try not to lose characteristic of my mall.

This machine should be able to have two faces. One way coexisting with the situation of the city mall and the other fighting against all and making noises, being fast, being very confusing in a way and then...back to the quiet life of being a good sculpture... A sculpture like Dr. Jekyll and Mr. Hyde."
   Jean Tinguely, 1972

1995 Yellow Neon Chandelier
Columbus Area Visitors Center, 506 5th Street

Dale Chihuly, *glass artist*
Seattle, Washington

This chandelier of 900 pieces of hand blown glass in four shades of yellow is nine feet tall and six feet across at the top. It is the only Chihuly piece in the country to be illuminated from inside, with 50 feet of neon tubing. Like many of the architects of Columbus, Chihuly was a relatively unknown artist when he was commissioned by J. Irwin and Xenia S. Miller.

1995 Persians
Facing Page
Columbus Area Visitors Center, 506 5th Street

Dale Chihuly, *glass artist*
Seattle, Washington

The name "Persians" was the artist whim, Chihuly felt the name fit the shapes of the wall-mounted pieces. The colorful hand-spun glass plates are attached to the bay window frame. The Chihuly sculptures were a gift from J. Irwin and Xenia S. Miller.

Sun Garden Panels
2007 in Suspended Circle
Columbus Learning Center, 4555 Central Ave.

Dale Chihuly, *glass artist*
Seattle, Washington

Dale Chihuly is renowned as an artist, as well as a glass sculptor. This piece is a combination of both, with 32 translucent white plexiglass panels boldly painted and signed, positioned under a round skylight. Each panel represents one of Chihuly's blown-glass forms. The sculpture was commissioned by Richard Johnson and family.

2006 Eos

5th Street, between Brown & Lindsey Streets

Dessa Kirk, artist
Chicago, Illinois

In Greek mythology, the winged Eos was the goddess of the dawn, and rose from her home at the edge of Oceanus, the Ocean, dispersed the mists of the night and opened the gates of heaven every day so her brother, Helios, the sun, could ride his chariot across the sky. Generally depicted as a supernaturally beautiful woman, her tears were considered to be the morning dew. Eos is one of the second generation of god and goddesses in Greek mythology called the Titans.

This sculpture was originally installed in 2006 in front of City Hall as a part of the Public Sculpture Invitational, it was later purchased by the community and permanently installed in a Fifth Street median strip facing the entry to Mill Race Park.

1979 Birds of Fire

The Republic, 2nd and Jackson Streets

Ted Sitting Crow Garner, sculptor
Chicago, Illinois

The bright orange steel sculpture was inspired from a poem by Sri Chinmoy. Part of the Public Sculpture Invitational, the sculpture was installed in 2006 and removed in 2012.

1979 Skopos
Mill Race Park

facing page

Rick Bauer, *sculptor*
San Francisco, California

Skopos, the Greek word loosely translated as "The Watcher", is a sculpture along the People Trails in Mill Race Park. The steel sculpture is imposing, with sleek curving lines.

1998 Crack the Whip
Corner of Brown and Second Street

Jo Saylors, *sculptor*
Ponca City, Oklahoma

The realistic bronze sculptures feature four kids playing a children's game. The piece is meticulous in detail, right down to the wrinkles in the clothes and the off-balance feel at the point of time depicted.

Formerly located on the site of the ArvinMeritor corporate headquarters, now the BSCS Administration Building, the sculpture was commissioned by Mr. and Mrs. James K. Baker in honor of ArvinMeritor employees.

1998 Puddles and Frog Pond
BCSC Administration Offices
2020 13th Street (Central Ave.)

Jo Saylors, *sculptor*
Ponca City, Oklahoma

The realistic bronze sculptures feature a boy leaning forward and a girl about to step into the water.

1987 2 Arcs de 212.5
The Commons, 300 Washington Street *facing page*

Bernar Venet, *sculptor*
Atelier Marioni, Vosges, France

Also called the "Red Cs", the double "C" sculpture is precariously balanced, this work reflects the artist's love of mathematics and his habit of investigating material, form, balance, and spatial perception.

2008 Jacob's Ladder
Hotel Indigo, 5th Street

Bernie Carreno, *sculptor*
Indianapolis, Indiana

The 14-foot metal sculpture is formally simple and abstract with a constructivist influence. The artist is known for his attention to form and color. Part of the Public Sculpture Invitational, the sculpture was installed in 2008.

2006 Summer Storm
Courthouse Square, 2nd and Washington Streets

Michael Helbing, *sculptor*
Chicago, Illinois

The three-dimensional expression of a summertime storm is influenced by the artist's experiences as a Vietnam veteran. The sculpture is appropriately located next to the Veteran's Memorial. Part of the Public Sculpture Invitational, the sculpture was installed in 2006, removed in 2012.

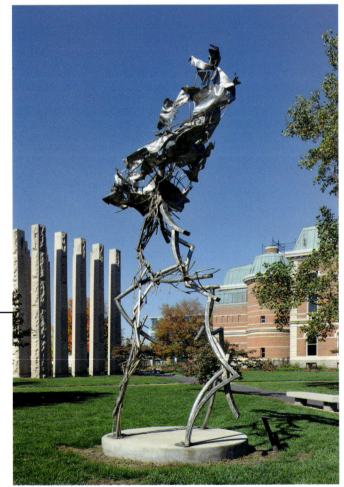

1997 Iris
Columbus Area Visitors Center, 506 5th Street

Scott Westphal, *sculptor*
Indianapolis, Indiana

This twisted aluminum sculpture used an I-beam design that represents an international symbol of strength. The artist's works are hybrids of abstraction, minimalism and figuration, with the I-beam his common theme. Part of the Public Sculpture Invitational, the sculpture was installed in 2008.

1998 Daquqi
Robert Garton Plaza, 2nd Street

Peter Lunderg, *sculptor*
Bosmoseen, Vermont

The nine-ton sculpture takes its name from a Rumi poem. The piece is created with concrete and circular patterned stainless steel. Part of the Public Sculpture Invitational, the sculpture was installed in 2006.

2006 Ancestral Way   *also on the facing page*
3rd Street, between Jackson and Lindsey Streets
2006

Robert Pulley, *sculptor*
Columbus, Indiana

Eleven organic forms appear in procession along the hillside as visitors exit the city. The hand-built stoneware fired ceramic sculptures combine references to the human figure with organic and geologic forms. Part of the Public Sculpture Invitational, the sculptures were installed in 2006.

1984 History-Mystery
facing page

City Hall, 123 Washington Street

William T. Wiley, *artist*
San Francisco, California

The mural in the tympanium of the council chamber dome, located on the second floor of City hall, depicts local history. The artist was an Indiana native, born in Bedford, Indiana.

1981 "C" wall hanging
City Hall Council Chamber, 123 Washington Street

Robert Indiana, *artist*
Vinalhaven, Maine

Robert Indiana, famous for the "LOVE" sculpture, once lived near Columbus in Elizabethtown.

City Hall murals
City Hall Council Chamber, 123 Washington Street

Four murals immortalize local citizens.
- **1999 Jack the Bum**
  Cathe Buris, *artist*
- **2000 Tommy Warner: a.k.a. Santa Claus**
  David Williams, *artist*
- **2002 Charles Kitzinger: Friend of the Orphans**
  Timothy Greatbatch, *artist*
- **2003 Carl Miske: The Head River Rat**
  Lyndia Burris, *artist*

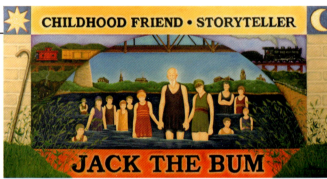

2002 Generations
below

Post Office, 200 Jackson Street

Betty Boyle, *artist*
Indianapolis, Indiana

Five painted panels show the progression of local architecture from the 1901 post office to the present. (3 panels shown below).

184

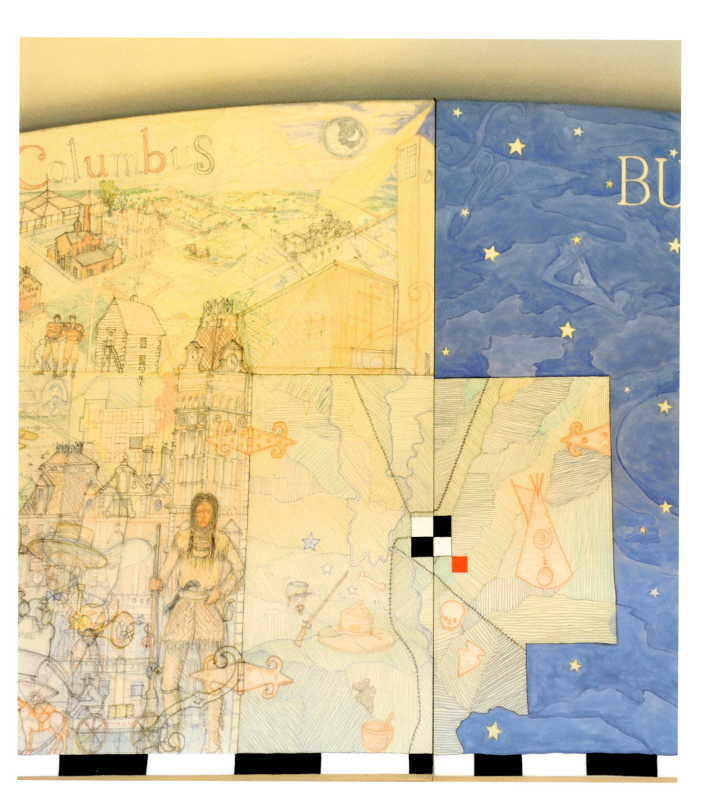

1984 Bronze Engine
Cummins Corporate Office Building
500 Jackson Street

The bronze sculpture outside the main building entry is the Cummins 16-cylinder KTA50 diesel engine.

1985 Exploded Engine *facing page*
Cummins Corporate Office Building Museum

Rudolph de Harak, *graphic artist / sculptor*
New York, New York

This is Cummins Big Cam III engine with more than 500 unique parts suspended on cables. The display was assembled entirely by Cummins employees over nine months, a celebration of teamwork.

Material Column
Cummins Corporate Office Building Museum

This 15-foot column shows all of the materials in the proportions in which they were used in a Cummins diesel engine during the late 1990s.

1934 Auburn
Cummins Corporate Office Building Museum

In 1934, Clessie Cummins worked with Auburn, an automobile manufacturer, to produce a few diesel-powered cars. Clessie used this car to promote the power, low cost and dependability of a diesel-powered car. This is the only remaining Cummins-powered Auburn.

2011 Halcyon
Columbus Regional Hospital, 2400 17th Street

facing page

Todd Frahm, *sculptor*
Solsberry, Indiana

This limestone sculpture illustrates a dove emerging from the flood. The piece was dedicated to mark the aftermath of the devastating 2008 flood. It was dedicated to the caring staff, physicians, and volunteers who endured the flood and worked to restore the hospital to working order. The sculpture was a gift from Xenia S. Miller.

1964 The Family
Parkside Elementary School courtyard
1400 Parkside Drive

Harris Barron, *sculptor*
Boston, Massachusetts

Located in the central courtyard of Parkside Elementary School, the Chelmsford granite sculpture was a gift to the community schools by Mrs. J. Irwin Miller through the Bartholomew Consolidated School Foundation. Three angular figures represent a father, mother and child. Children climb upon and interact with the forms.

1998 Celebration
Foundation for Youth, 400 North Cherry Street

Gary Price, *sculptor*
Springville, Utah

Located in the lobby of the Foundation for Youth, this whimsical bronze sculpture features children in flight.

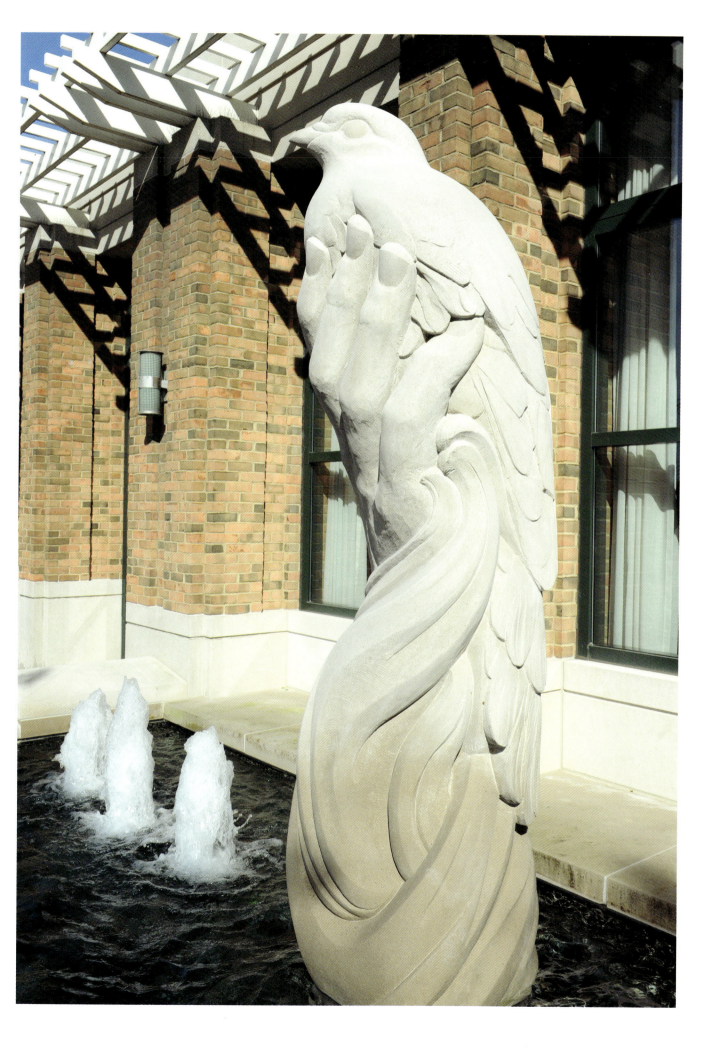

2012 Transformation

facing page

Indiana University Purdue University Columbus
4601 Central Ave.

Howard Meehan, artist
Santa Fe, New Mexico

A 30-foot tall stainless steel sculpture with three rods of lighted glass and a steel ring. The surrounding concrete wall features a quote by Benjamin Disraeli: "A University Must be a Place of Light, of Liberty, and of Learning."

2005 Self-Made Man

Columbus Learning Center
4601 Central Ave.

Bobbie Carlye, sculptor
Colorado

"Man carving himself out of stone, carving his character, carving his future." The sculpture was dedicated in honor of John T. Hackett.

2007 Discovery

Indiana University - Purdue University Columbus
4601 Central Ave.

Kusser Granitwerke
Germany

"Discovery" suggests undefined possibilities both internally through reading and reflection, and externally through the world around us. The kinetic nature of the piece itself is a reminder that the pursuit of "discovery" is never ending.

This sculpture is a kugel, from the German word for "ball", that combines water and stone. The three foot diameter, 2,300 pound ball is carved from South African New Belfast black granite, kept in motion by 12 pounds of water pressure. Each of the three books are made from a different type of granite from the Bavarian Forest in Germany.

2006 Yellowwood Coral *facing page*
Bartholomew Country Recycling Center
Mapleton Street

Lucy Slivinski, artist
Chicago, Illinois

The sculpture contains scrap metal from Columbus and bike frames from Chicago. The work was inspired by fungal formations the artist encountered while hiking the Yellowwood Forest west of Columbus. Part of the Public Sculpture Invitational, the sculpture was originally located in 2006 on the lawn of City Hall.

2006 Freedom Field sculptures
Freedom Field, Blackwell Park
behind Parkside Elementary School, 1400 Parkside Dr.

Amy Lienhoop, Mark Thompson
Columbus, Indiana

2000 Hamilton Center sculpture
Hamilton Center, Lincoln Park, 2501 25th Street

Dale Patterson, art instructor
Malcom Stalcup, welding instructor
Columbus North High School students
Columbus, Indiana

This was a collaborative effort over a six year period with teachers and students at Columbus North High School. Art students worked on the design while welding students did the construction of the 18-foot tall sculpture with the cor-ten steel elements. The art students learned basic welding and the welding students learned art. Columbus North technology students poured the concrete base.

1989 "When I Was Your Age"
Faurecia, 950 West 450 South, Walesboro

J. Seward Johnson, Jr., artist
Santa Monica, California

The realistic sculpture was originally located at the traffic circle on 13th Street and Hutchson Ave., commissioned by Arvin Industries to display their first product, a tire pump, in front of their headquarters. The bronze sculpture was cast using a real car. The clothing is real, preserved using a patina and lacquer process developed by the artist.

2011 Luckey Climber
The Commons, 300 Washington Street

Tom Luckey, *artist & architect*
Spencer Luckey, *installer*
Luckey, LLC
East New Haven, Connecticut

The Luckey Climber is the featured playground piece of the new playground at The Commons. When Copley Wolff Design Group was conducting workshops with the kids of Columbus to see what they wanted in their new custom designed playground, the response was "climbers, mazes, tunnels and slides." The Luckey Climber seems to fulfill all of those elements in one.

Designed by Tom Luckey, an architect and artist, and installed by his son Spencer, these unique climbing structures are located throughout the United States and Mexico. Structurally supported by 5 steel columns, 50 custom designed and fabricated curved plywood platforms interconnect to create a unique play experience. The platforms are connected with six miles of coated stainless steel aircraft cable to provide additional support and a netting to create a safe climbing structure.

Elegantly set in the crystalline playground pavilion, the Luckey Climber is simultaneously the community's latest piece of public art and a twenty-first century jungle gym that may earn the new playground the name of "Chaos No. 2" again. The custom designed playground structure was a gift from the Irwin-Sweeney-Miller Foundation.

photos by Susan Fleck

photos by Susan Fleck

1974 Dancing "C"

Paul Rand, *graphic artist*
New York, New York

In 1962 Paul Rand, one of America's premier graphic artist, created the trademarked corporate logo and identity for Cummins Engine Company. Among his noteworthy designs are iconic logos for ABC, Westinghouse, IBM and UPS. He was a graphic consultant for Cummins from 1961-1996.

For the Columbus Area Visitors Center, he created the colorful "dancing Cs" (1974), letterhead, signs, visitors maps, architectural tour markers, and designed the first editions of this book from 1978 to 1991, including its covers. The cover shown is the first edition.

In 2006, the Columbus Brand Committee worked with North Star Destination Strategies from Nashville, TN, to create the community brand, "unexpected. unforgettable.", which included the logo with a skewed "C" based on Paul Rand's original design and his modern typography. This logo has been incorporated in several designs including the Luckey Climber, the fritted glass at The new Commons, and the bike racks located throughout the city.

A Look
At Architecture

Columbus
Indiana

Two themes have been identified in the development of Columbus and Bartholomew County as a Nationally-significant center of Modern architecture, Patronage in Public Architecture (1957-1973), and Modern Architecture and Landscape Architecture (1942-1973.)

The Patronage in Public Architecture theme is represented by local business support of outstanding Modern architecture and landscape. Cummins Engine Company Foundation established a program in the 1950s to pay the design fees for local, public projects if the client group selected the design firm from a list developed by an independent panel of experts. Since the program started, many public resources have been constructed. In addition, the patronage program fostered an outstanding design sensibility in the community, resulting in private sector construction on additional Modern architecture resources. Programs that promote Modern architecture in this way are rare in the United States. Columbus' program may be the most extensive, long-term program of its kind.

The Modern Architects and Landscape Architecture theme is represented by an exceptional collection of significant Modern buildings, landscapes, and public sculpture that reflects the development of these design idioms on a national basis. Many of the designers experimented with concepts and design forms in Columbus that they then applied to larger and more famous works elsewhere. These cultural resources reflect design trends of the period in which they were constructed in response to a quest for excellence in design and creative problem solving. There is a broad cross-section of designers represented, rather than a collection of works by a small group. The comprehensive consideration of Modern architecture and landscape architecture, and the way in which the urban form has been shaped translates into an experience of national importance.

Executive Summary
National Historic Landmark Theme Study
1999

Laura Thayer, *architectural historian*
Margaret Storrow, *landscape architect*
John Kinsella, *urban designer*
Louis Joyner, *architect*
Malcolm Cairns, *landscape architect*

Historic Architecture in Columbus, Indiana

The exquisite historic buildings of Columbus, with their preservation, restoration, or renovations, sometimes with additions, are as important to the architectural character of this community as is the modern design.

In 1982, the **Columbus Historic District** was listed with the National Register of Historic Places, with almost 600 homes and commercial buildings. Ninety-one buildings were considered outstanding contributions, representing a variety of architectural styles including Federal, Italianate, Victorian, Second-Empire, late 19th century Queen Anne, Colonial Revival, Prairie, Cross Plan and Shot Gun workers' homes, Stick Style and Carpenter Gothic.

In a highly unusual move, the even more exclusive **National Historic Landmarks** program honored the city in 2000 by accepting six modern architectural and landscape architecture sites simultaneously. The seventh was designated in 2012. See National Recognition of Columbus, Indiana.

The **National Trust for Historic Preservation** named Columbus, Indiana to the 2005 list of the Dozen Distinctive Destinations in the U.S.

National Geographic Traveler, in their Nov/Dec 2008 edition ranked Columbus **11th out of 109 historic destinations worldwide by National Geographic Society's Center for Sustainable Destinations**, higher than any other U.S. destination. The magazine says Columbus has "a world-class collection of modern architecture by master architects... it is authentic, unique, and unspoiled ... this town is truly part of America's architectural heritage."

1874 Bartholomew County Courthouse
Third & Washington Streets

Isaac Hodgson
Indianapolis, Indiana

The Second Empire-style building has been recognized as one of the most beautiful county courthouses in the state and is said to be the first fire-proof building in Indiana. It was featured on the cover of the book *The Magnificent 92 Indiana Courthouses.*

The courthouse continues to serve its original civic purpose well and stands much the same as it did when it was originally designed, even with several renovations throughout the years. Most of the original interior spaces have been preserved, including the marble and terrazzo floors, wood trim, fireplaces and a spiral staircase. An elevator was added in 1998 to provide convenience and accessibility. The original slate roof was replaced with copper in 1952. The delicate, lightweight grillwork on the three towers was added in 1971, a gift from Elsie Irwin Sweeney. Award-winning landscape architect Michael Van Valkenburgh developed a master plan for landscape plantings for the Courthouse Square. The building is listed on the National Register of Historic Places.

1864 Irwin House & Garden
608 Fifth Street
1864 original, 1880 and 1910 remodeling

1910 Henry Phillips
Boston, Massachusetts

Built in 1864 by Joseph I. Irwin, Columbus banker and businessman, this Italianate design was remodeled in 1880. However, to accommodate four generations of the Irwin family, the home has been enlarged and redesigned over the years. The current mansion was the achievement of Henry A. Phillips, a Massachusetts architect, who was hired by William G. Irwin in 1910. The intricate detail of the extensive fine woodwork and moldings throughout the house are reminiscent of a European estate. The old brick exterior was covered by tapestry brick with stone trim, and several new chimneys, which are now a prominent feature of the house, were added. The roof was recovered in slate and the pitch was altered, providing for a more spacious third floor. On the east, a raised terrace was added to link the home to the adjoining Garden.

The highlight of this two-acre property is the garden, a beautiful maze based on the Casa degli Innamorati in Pompeii. Several fountains and a long pool are the focal point of a lowered sunken garden. There is a statue under the center arch of the garden house designed from a lakeside structure at the Villa of Hadrian at Tivoli, Italy. Pompeian murals accent the garden house. A tall brick wall is rounded in imitation of 16th-century gardens in Mantua, Italy. Wisteria vines on the terrace's pergolas were planted in 1911, and continue to bloom in the spring. Only the English sundial and a Japanese bronze elephant sculpture that is a replica of one at the 1904 St. Louis World's Fair pavilion do not follow the Italian motif.

The House and Gardens is currently operated as a bed and breakfast inn.

1884 Ruddick-Nugent House
1210 16th Street

1924 Charles F. Sparrell
Columbus, Indiana

The original house 1884 Queen Anne house was renovated in 1924 to create its current Greek Revival style, with the tall front columns. The House is currently operated as a bed and breakfast inn.

Bartholomew Country Historic Society
1864
524 Third Street

facing page

1973 Renovation
Dean Taylor
Columbus, IN

Originally built for William McEwen, it was bought in 1870 by Daniel Samuels who added the front addition that turned the home into a Victorian house. James and Mary Marr occupied the house until 1916. The house was renovated for the Bartholomew County Historic Society.

1853 Franklin Square
1870 538 Franklin Street

1970 Renovation

Franklin Square is a quarter block that that consists of a Federal style house, built in 1853 for Samuel Harris and an Italianate style house, built in 1870 for Dr. William Hogue. The houses were renovated in 1970, including the offices of the Heritage Fund - the Community Foundation of Bartholomew County.

1895 Old City Hall
445 Fifth Street, corner of Franklin Street

Charles F. Sparrell
Columbus, Indiana

1986 Renovation into the Columbus Inn.
2012 Renovation into apartments.

Built in the Romanesque style, the building features a tall bell tower and stone arched entries. The building is listed on the National Register of Historic Places.

1925 The Armory
641 Franklin Street

1973 Renovation into senior housing.
Browning Day Mullins Dierdorf (BDMD)
Indianapolis, Indiana.

1896 Maple Grove - Garfield School
One Norbitt Plaza

Charles F. Sparrell
Columbus, Indiana

1989 Addition and renovation
Ratio Architects
Indianapolis, Indiana

The Romanesque Revival school building was originally built with four classrooms, with a planned expansion to eight classrooms. The design was unique with a variety of flat and arched vertical windows, featuring a central bell tower and a stone arched entry. The addition and renovation converted the school into a company headquarters for Arvin Industries, including a sunken garden. The building is currently occupied by the Bartholomew County School Corporation administrative offices.

1891 Prall House
605 Fifth Street (corner of Lafayette Street)

Charles F. Sparrell
Columbus, Indiana

1989 Renovation
Dean Taylor
Columbus, IN

A Queen Anne Victorian house.

1892 McKinley School
3301 McKinley Avenue

Charles F. Sparrell
Columbus, Indiana

1988 Renovation into apartments

This Romanesque Revival style school was originally called North Side.

1896 Power House
148 Lindsey Street

Harrison Albright
Charlestown, West Virginia

1975 Renovation - Senior Center
James K. Paris
Columbus, Indiana

Water pumps and dynomos once generated electricity for the city from this distinctive brick building located on the banks of the White River. The building is listed on the National Register of Historic Places.

1900 Zaharakos
329 Washington Street

facing page

2009 Renovation and expansion

For more than 100 years, this popular ice cream parlor was known as Zaharako's Confectionery. Founded by three brothers from Greece, this establishment was family owned until 2006.

Zaharakos Ice Cream Parlor and Museum reopened after three years of extensive renovation by a local businessman, preserving the smallest detail. The original onyx soda fountain, with an Italian marble countertop, came from the 1904 St. Louis Exposition & World's Fair. The 184 pipe mechanical, full-concert organ, imported from Freiburg, Germany in 1908 still plays. The original space has expanded into the adjacent building to create a museum space with a second soda fountain and additional seating.

For architectural enthusiasts, this is the place J. Irwin Miller frequently met and became friends with Eero Saarinen.

1965 Storefront Improvements
Downtown Columbus, Indiana

Alexander Girard
Santa Fe, New Mexico

"Storefront renovation has been one of the important elements of the re-awakened interest in a lively downtown Columbus. It was a simple idea, and a very good one!" After meeting and doing a "looking-up" walking tour with downtown business owners and tenants, Girard talked about capitalizing on the one major architectural asset of the central business area, the wealth of Victorian detail. He proposed painting the deteriorated buildings from a color concept of 26 colors, including bright accent colors to appeal to young people. A uniform canopy over sidewalks and suggested signs, some whimsical to represent the type of business.

The design concept was presented on masonite panels, currently on display at City Hall. A model block was completed on Washington Street, between 5th and 6th Streets in 1965. Over the years, about 80 percent of the storefronts have been renovated.

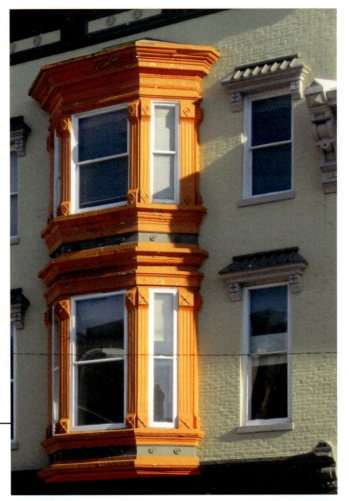

1941 Fire Station No. 1
1101 Jackson (Washington) Street

facing page

Leighton Bowers
Indianapolis, IN

1990 Addition & renovation
James Paris, Nolan Bingham
Architect Group, Columbus, IN

The original art deco fire station faced Washington Street with curved glass corners and a round hose tower. The addition related the apparatus room to face 11th Street, with a sensitive two-story addition.

1942 Crump Theater
1889 425 Third Street

Charles F. Sparrell
Columbus, Indiana

1934 The art deco facade, featuring the marquee, curved glass entry and the 'vitrolite' pigmented glass front,
1942 was the result of a 1942 renovation. The original 1889 building featured 3 arches, was designed by Charles Sparrell as an opera house which was an addition to an earlier commercial building. The 1934 renovation largely defines the existing auditorium style.

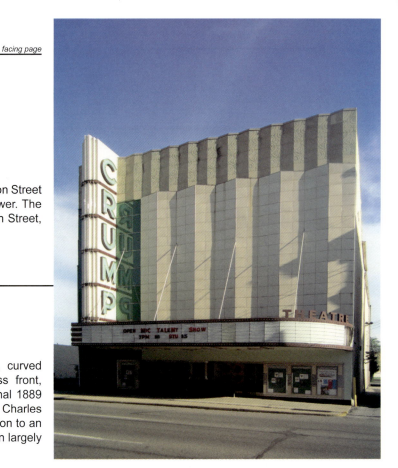

2005 kidscommons
309 Washington Street

Louis Joyner
Louis Joyner, Architect
Columbus, Indiana

exhibit designer / consultants
Louis Joyner
Quatrefoil Exhibit Designers, Maryland
Cincinnati Children's Museum

Kidscommons is Columbus' community children's museum. Located in a two-story brick building once occupied by J.C. Penney Department Store, the renovated building includes three floors of interactive exhibits for fun and learning. The new entry features a kid-sized entrance door that uses custom pulls to create a face and is surrounded by a wall composed of children's wooden blocks. The facade is enlivened with three abstract figures of children climbing the wall.

Several popular exhibits include a 17-foot tall climbing wall referencing the building facade, a Japanese house, a Childrenhood Garden, and a giant toilet that kids can slide down.

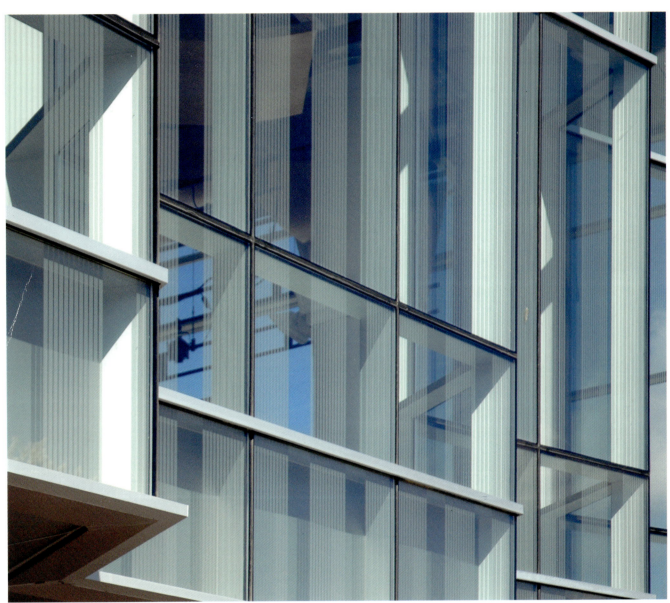
The Commons *(photo by Jennifer Risting)*

Appendix

TIMELINE of selected Architecture, Landscape Architecture and Art......................214-217

Architects / Landscape Architects / Artists...218-223
    and their works in Columbus, Indiana
    with brief bibliography: education, collaboration and selected publications

Modern Architecture & Public Art..224-225
    listed alphabetically with location

Columbus, Indiana Contractors.. 226
    contribution to excellence

Columbus, Indiana map... 227
    of major architectural sites

Acknowledgements / Credits...228

TIMELINE of selected Architecture, Landscape Architecture and Art

The major buildings and projects, including historic buildings, modern buildings, master plans, landscape architecture and public art are listed chronologically, based on the buildings completion date. The building / project names are original, with current names noted with the project narratives.

*The **bolded** projects are included in this book. Additions are noted with the original project date and the date they were completed, while often illustrated in the book, they are not bolded. The dates are based upon the previous book editions, and corrected based upon additional research when possible. See project narratives for dates when projects began design.*

The leading design architect, architectural firm, landscape architect, or artist is listed, with key contributing designers noted with the project narratives. Architect's and landscape architect's design fees supported by The Cummins Foundation Architecture Program are noted with (CF).

Year	Building / Project	Architect / Artist	Page
	Historic Architecture and renovations		
1853	**Harris House** (Franklin Square)		204
	1970 renovation		
1864	**McEwen House** (Bartholomew Co. Historical Society)		204
	1973 renovation	Dean Taylor	
1864	**Irwin House and Gardens**		202
	1910 renovation	Henry Phillips	
1864	**Storey House** (Columbus Area Visitors Center)		122
	1973 renovation	Bruce Adams	
	1995 addition & renovation	Kevin Roche	
	2012-2013 interior renovations	Jonathan Hess	
1870	Pollert House		
	1997 renovation		
1870	**Hogue House** (Franklin Square)		204
	1970 renovation		
1871	James Marr House and Farm		
1874	**Bartholomew County Courthouse**	Isaac Hodgson	200
	1969 renovation	SIECO, Inc.	
	1998 renovation	Charles Budd	
1875	First Presbyterian Church		
	1981 renovation	IDS, Inc.	
1881	**Irwin Management Company** (301 Washington Street)		72
	1972 renovation	Alexander Girard	
	2012 interior renovation	David Force	
1884	**Ruddick-Nugent House**	Charles Sparrell	202
	1924 renovation		
1885	Irwin Union Capital Corporation (Fehring building)	Charles Sparrell	
	1989 renovation	Kevin Roche	
1886	Nelson Bible Mart		
	1996 renovation		
1887	Marr-Lucas Building		
1889	**Crump Theater**	Charles Sparrell	210
	1922, 1932, 1942 renovations		
1890	Elnora Daugherty Farm		
1891	**Prall House**	Charles Sparrell	206
	1986 renovation	Dean Taylor	
1892	**McKinley School** (North Side School)		206
1895	**Old City Hall**	Charles Sparrell	204
	1986 renovation (Columbus Inn)		
	2012 renovation (apartments)		
1896	**Maple Grove School**	Charles Sparrell	206
	1989 addition and renovation (Arvin Headquarters)	Ratio Architects	
	2002 renovation (BCSC Administration)		
1900	**Zaharako's confectionery**		208
	2010 renovation (Ice Cream Parlor & Museum)		
1901	**Power House**	Harrison Albright	206
	1976 renovation (Senior Center)	James Paris	
1910	**Irwin Garden** remodeling	Henry Phillips (landscape)	202
1925	**The Armory**		204
	1995 renovation (senior housing)	BDMD	
1932	**Elephant** sculpture		168
1941	**Fire Station #1**	Leighton Bowers	210
	1990 addition and renovations	James Paris, Nolan Bingham	

TIMELINE of selected Architecture, Landscape Architecture and Art

Year	Building / Project	Architect / Artist	Page

Modern Architecture

Year	Building / Project	Architect / Artist	Page
1942	**First Christian Church** (2000 addition)	Eliel Saarinen	20
1953	Columbus Village apartments (3 phases -1960)	Harry Weese	
1953	Bassett House	Harry Weese	
1953	Lauther House	Harry Weese	
1954	**Irwin Union Bank**	Eero Saarinen	22
1954	Boys and Girls Club (demolished)	Harry Weese	
1957	**Miller House and Garden**	Eero Saarinen / Alexander Girard (interiors) / Dan Kiley (landscape)	24
1957	**Lillian C. Schmitt Elementary School** (1991 addition)	Harry Weese (CF)	28
1958	**Lincoln Center** (Hamilton Center Ice Arena) (1975 additon)	Harry Weese	30
1958	**Hope, IN branch bank**	Harry Weese (Ben Weese)	32
1959	Salvation Army Corps Community Center	Harry Weese	
1960	Cummins Engine Plant One additions	Harry Weese	124
1960	**Mabel McDowell Adult Education Center** (Originally elementary school)	John Carl Warnecke (CF)	34
1961	**Northside Middle School** (1991 addition)	Harry Weese (Ben Weese) (CF)	36
1961	**Eastbrook Plaza branch bank** (1996 addition)	Harry Weese	38
1961	State Street branch bank & Shopping Center	Harry Weese (Ben Weese)	
1962	**Cosco Inc. Office Building**	Harry Weese / Dan Kiley (landscape)	40
1962	**Parkside Elementary School** (1990 addition)	Norman Fletcher (TAC) (CF)	42
1963	**BCSC Administration Building**	Norman Fletcher (TAC) (CF)	44
1964	**North Christian Church**	Eero Saarinen / Dan Kiley (landscape)	46
1964	Newlin House	Harry Weese	
1964	**"The Family"** sculpture	Harris Barron	188
1964	**Otter Creek Clubhouse and Golf Course** (1995 golf course addition) (2010 scoreboard)	Harry Weese (CF) / Dan Kiley (landscape) / Robert Trent Jones (golf course) (CF)	48
1965	**First Baptist Church**	Harry Weese / Dan Kiley (landscape)	50
1965	**W.D. Richards Elementary School** (1997 addition)	Edwards Larrabee Barnes (AP) / Dan Kiley (landscape)	52
1965	Cummins Engine Plant One additions	Harry Weese	124
1965	Downtown Storefront renovation project	Alexander Girard	208
1966	Taylorsville branch bank	Fisher and Spillman / Dan Kiley (landscape)	
1967	**Four Seasons Retirement Center**	Norman Fletcher (TAC) (AP)	54
1967	**Lincoln Elementary School**	Gunnar Birkerts (AP) / Johnson, Johnson & Roy (JJR) (landscape)	56
1968	**Fire Station No. 4**	Robert Venturi (CF)	58
1968	**Cummins Technical Center** (1997 renovation)	Harry Weese / Dan Kiley (landscape)	60
1968	Downtown Master Plan	SOM	
1969	**Cleo Rogers Memorial Library** (B.C. Public Library) (1987 addition)	I.M. Pei	62
1969	**L. Frances Smith Elementary School** (1997 addition and renovation)	John Johansen (CF)	64
1969	**Southside Elementary School** Murals, Ivan Chermayeff	Eliot Noyes (CF)	66
1970	**U.S. Post Office - Columbus**	Kevin Roche (CF)	68
1971	**"Large Arch"** sculpture	Henry Moore	170
1971	**The Republic**	Myron Goldsmith (SOM)	70
1972	**301 Washington St.** facade & interiors	Alexander Girard	72
1972	**Columbus East High School** (1998 gym addition) (2012 addition and renovation)	Romaldo Giurgola (MGA) (CF)	74
1972	**Mt. Healthy Elementary School** (2002 addition)	Hugh Hardy (HHPA) (CF)	76

TIMELINE of selected Architecture, Landscape Architecture and Art

Year	Building / Project	Architect / Artist	Page
1972	**Par 3 Golf Course Clubhouse**	Bruce Adams (CF)	78
1972	**Quinco Consulting Center** (Mental Health Center)	James Polshek (CF)	80
1972	**Irwin Union Bank & Trust Co. Office Building** 2012 Renovation	Kevin Roche	82
1973	The Commons and Commons Mall (demolished)	Cesar Pelli (Gruen)	162
1973	Washington Street Plan (project)	Laurence Alexander	
1973	Storey House renovated for Visitors Center	Bruce Adams	
1973	**Cummins Occupational Health Association** (Cummins Health Center)	Hugh Hardy (HHPA) Dan Kiley (landscape)	84
1973	**Cummins Sub-Assembly Plant** (Midrange Engine)	Kevin Roche	86
1973	**Fodrea Community School** 2010 Renovation	Paul Kennon (CRS) (CF)	88
1974	**"Chaos I"**	Jean Tinguely	172
1974	City Power House converted to Senior Center	James Paris	206
1974	**State Street branch bank**	Paul Kennon (CRS) Dan Kiley (landscape)	90
1975	Hamilton Center Ice Arena addition	Koster & Associates	30
1978	**Indiana Bell Switching Center** (AT&T)	Paul Kennon (CRS)	92
1979	**"Skopos"** sculpture	Rick Bauer	178
1981	**Columbus City Hall**	Edward Charles Bassett (SOM) (CF)	94
1982	**CERAland Recreation Center**	Harry Roth (Roth and Moore)	96
1982	**Clifty Creek Elementary School** 1997 addition	Richard Meier (CF)	98
1982	**Sycamore Place**	Charles Gwathmey (G-SA)(CF)	100
1983	Downtown Master Plan	SOM	
1984	**Cummins Corporate Office Building** "Exploded Engine"	Kevin Roche Jack Curtis (landscape)	102
1984	**Pence Place Apartments**	Charles Gwathmey (G-SA)(CF)	104
1987	**Fire Station No. 5**	Susana Torre (CF)	106
1987	Cleo Rogers Memorial Library addition	James Paris	62
1987	**"2 Arc de 212.5"** sculpture	Bernar Venet	180
1988	**St. Peter's Lutheran Church**	Gunnar Birkerts	108
1998	Downtown concept planning	Paul Kennon (CRSS)	
1989	**Hope Elementary School**	Taft Architects (CF)	110
1989	"When I Was Your Age" sculpture	J. Seward Johnson, Jr.	192
1990	**Bartholomew County Jail** 2008 addition	Don Hisaka (CF)	112
1990	Parkside Elementary School addition	Norman Fletcher (TAC) (CF)	42
1990	**Streetscape** Parking lots	Paul Kennon (CRSS) (CF) Michael Van Valkenburgh	114
1990	Mill Race Connected Parks & Golf Course (project)	Michael Van Valkenburgh (landscape) Paul Kennon (CRSS)	
1991	Lillian C. Schmitt Elementary School addition	Leers/Weinzapfel(CF)	28
1991	Northside Middle School addition	Leers/Weinzapfel(CF)	36
1992	**Columbus Regional Hospital expansion**	Robert A.M. Stern (CF)	116
1992	**Mill Race Park** Park Structures Stanley Saitowitz (CF)	Michael Van Valkenburgh (landscape) (CF)	118
1993	Gateway Study (project)(partially competed)	Robert Venturi, Steven Izenour Michael Van Valkenburgh (landscape)	126
1993	IMA-Columbus Gallery (demolished at Commons)	Todd Williams	
1993	Streetscape (Phase 2)	CRSS (CF)	
1993	Bartholomew County Courthouse Square	Michael Van Valkenburgh (landscape) (CF)	
1995	**Breeden Realtors Office building**	Thomas Beeby, Gary Ainge	120
1995	**Visitors Center addition & renovation**	Kevin Roche Jack Curtis (landscape)	122
1991	Otter Creek Golf Course expansion	Rees Jones	48
1995	**"Yellow Neon Chandelier" and Persians"**	Dale Chihuly	174
1996	Eastbrook Plaza branch bank addition	Thomas Beeby, Gary Ainge	38
1996	**Cummins Columbus Engine Plant addition**	Kevin Roche Jack Curtis (landscape)	12
1997	**Gateway bridge (I-65)**	Jean Muller	126
1997	**Bartholomew County Veterans Memorial**	Thompson and Rose (CF)	128
1997	**The Republic Printing Center**	GSI (Forum Architects)	130

TIMELINE of selected Architecture, Landscape Architecture and Art

Year	Building / Project	Architect / Artist	Page
1997	W.D. Richards Elementary School addition	John M.Y. Lee (CF)	52
1997	Clifty Creek Elementary School addition	Stamberg Aferiat Architecture (CF)	98
1997	Cummins Technical Center renovation	HOK	60
1997	L. Frances Smith Elementary School addition	Christian Johansen, John Johansen (CF)	64
1998	**Fire Station No. 6**	William Rawn (CF)	132
1998	**"Friendship Way"** Downtown Alley Walkway Projects	William Johnson	134
1998	**Hope Library**	Deborah Burke (CF)	136
1998	East High School Gym addition	Mitchell-Giurgola (CF)	74
1998	Foundation for Youth	HOK	
1998	**"Celebration"** sculpture	Gary Price	188
1998	**"Crack the Whip"** sculpture	Jo Saylor	178
1998	**"Puddles and Frog Pond"** sculpture	Jo Saylor	178
1999	**Second Street bridge**	Jean Muller	126
2001	**Cummins Child Development Center** (2004 addition)	Carlos Jimenez	138
2001	**West Hill Plaza branch bank**	Carlos Jimenez	140
2002	**St. Paul's Episcopal Church renovation**	Thomas Beeby	142
2002	**St. Bartholomew Roman Catholic Church**	Steven Risting (Ratio)	144
2002	Mt. Healthy Elementary School addition	Nolan Bingham	76
2002	First Christian Church Addition	Nolan Bingham	20
2003	ArvinMeritor Columbus Technology Center	Robert W. Carrington (Ghafari Assoc.)	
2004	Cummins Childcare Center addition	Carlos Jimenez	138
2005	**Columbus Learning Center**	Kevin Kennon (KPF) (CF)	146
2005	**"Self-Made Man"** sculpture	Bobbie Carlye	190
2005	**Kidscommons**	Louis Joyner	210
2006	**Creekview branch bank**	Deborah Berke (CF)	148
2006	Freedom Field		42
2006	**Freedom Field** sculptures		192
2006	Mt. Healthy Elementary School addition	Nolan Bingham	76
2006	Public Sculpture Invitational		
	"Eos", 2006 sculpture	Dessa Kirk	176
	"Birds of Fire", 1979 sculpture	Ted Sitting Crow Garner	176
	"Summer Storm"	Michael Helbing	180
	"Daquqi", 1998 sculpture	Peter Lundig	182
	"Ancestral Way" sculptures	Robert Pulley	182
	"Yellowwood Coral"	Lucy Slivinski	192
2007	**Central Middle School**	Ralph Johnson (Perkins+Will) (CF)/CSO	150
2007	**"Sun Garden Panels in Suspended Circle"**	Dale Chihuly	174
2007	**"Discovery"** sculpture	Kusser Granitwerke	190
2008	Bartholomew County Jail addition	RQAW	112
2008	Public Sculpture Invitational		
	"Jacob's Ladder" sculpture	Bernie Carreno	180
	"Iris", 1997 sculpture	Scott Westphal	182
2009	**Jackson Street Parking Garage**	Koetter Kim (CF)	152
2009	**Commons Office Building** (for Cummins) (2012 addition)	CSO/Koetter Kim	154
2009	**Third Street Parking Garage**	Steven Risting (CSO)	156
2009	Jackson Place condominiums	Sam Miller (Solistice)	
2010	Otter Creek Golf Course Scoreboard	Kevin Roche	48
2010	Fodrea Community School renovation	CSO	88
2010	**"Transformation"** sculpture	Howard Meehan	190
2011	**Mill Race Center**	William Rawn (CF)	158
2011	**Advanced Manufacturing Center**	Cesar Pelli (CF)	160
2011	**The Commons**	Koetter Kim (CF)/CSO	162
2011	**"Luckey Climber"**	Tom Luckey	194
2011	**"Halcyon"** sculpture	Todd Frahm	188
2012	East High School addition and renovation	CSO	74
2012	North High School additions and renovation	CSO	
2012	Commons Office Building expansion	CSO/Koetter Kim	154
2012	**Cummins Parking Garage**	StructurePoint (Todd Williams/Kevin Roche)	164
2013	The Cole apartments	Steven Risting (CSO)	156
2014	Urban Elements apartments	Steven Risting (CSO)	164

Architects / Landscape Architects / Artists   and their works in Columbus, Indiana

Architects, Architectural Firms (name when commissioned), Landscape Architects and Artists and their projects (built and unbuilt) in Columbus, including selected bibliography.
National architects and artists **bold**, * *indicates project featured in this book.*

Architect / Landscape Architect / Artist   *Building / Project / Artwork*

Adams, Brewster (Bruce).................................Schmitt Elementary School, 1957 (*with* Harry Weese office)*
Bruce Adams-designer, New Haven, CT   Lincoln Center (Hamilton Center Ice Arena), 1958 (*with* Harry Weese office)*
worked for Eero Saarinen   Cummins General Office Building, 1970
worked for Harry Weese   Par 3 Clubhouse, 1972*
Yale University professor   Columbus Visitors Center, renovation of John Storey house, 1973

Adams, Frank Jr. (1940-2003).............................Developmental Service, Inc. (DSI) building, 1980
Frank Adams Jr. & Associates, Columbus, IN   Columbus Municipal Airport Terminal, 1983
                                                  IUPUC Columbus (building renovation), 1985

Ainge, Gary M...Eastbrook branch bank addition & renovation, 1996*
Hammond Beeby Babka, Chicago, IL   Breeden Realty Office Building, 1995*
                                                  St. Paul's Episcopal Church renovation, 2002

Albright, Harrison (1866-1933)..........................Power Plant, 1901
Charleston, West Virginia   West Baden Hotel, 1902

Barnes, Edward Larrabee (1915-2004)....................W.D. Richards Elementary School, 1965*
Edward Larrabee Barnes and Associates, New York, NY
Harvard University Graduate School of Design, 1942
<u>Edward Larrabee Barnes: Architect</u>, Rizzoli, 1994

Barron, Harris (b.1926) *sculptor*..........................."The Family", 1964*
Boston, MA

Bassett, Edward Charles (1921-1999).....................Columbus City Hall, 1981*
Skidmore, Owings & Merrill (SOM), San Francisco, CA
Cranbrook Academy of Art, 1951
worked for Eero Saarinen

Bauer, Richard *sculptor*......................................"Skopos", 1979*
Brookline, MA

Beeby, Thomas (b.1941)..................................Eastbrook branch bank addition & renovation, 1996*
Hammond Beeby Babka, Chicago, IL   Breeden Realty Office Building, 1995*
Yale University, 1965   St. Paul's Episcopal Church renovation, 2002*
Yale University, *dean of* School of Architecture, 1985-1991
Executive Architect to coordinate downtown planning

Berke, Deborah (b.1954)..................................Hope Library, 1998*
Deborah Berke Partners, New York, NY   Creekview Branch Bank (Irwin Union), 2006*
Yale University professor
<u>Deborah Berke</u>, Yale University Press, 2008

Bingham, Nolan (b.1946)...................................Fire Station No. 1 addition, 1990*
Paris Bingham Architects, Columbus, IN   B.C. Veterans Memorial, 1997* (*owner's representative*)
                                                  Pence Place family housing, 1984* (*consultant to* Gwathmey & Siegel Assoc.)
                                                  Ivy Tech Community College
                                                  First Christian Church addition, 2000
                                                  Mt. Healthy School addition, 2006*

Birkerts, Gunnar (b.1925).................................Lincoln Elementary School, 1967*
Gunnar Birkerts and Associates, Birmingham, MI   St. Peter's Lutheran Church, 1988*
worked for Eero Saarinen   Lincoln Elementary School addition, 2000 (not built)
<u>The Architecture of Gunnar Birkerts</u>, AIA Press, 1989
<u>Gunnar Birkerts: Projects and Thoughts 1960-1985</u>,
   Univ. of Michigan, 1985

Bowers, Leighton (1894-1944)..............................Columbus Fire Station No. 1, 1941*
Leighton Bowers Architect, Indianapolis, IN

Bolye, Betty *artist*.."Generations", 2002*
Indianapolis, IN

Budd, Charles J...Bartholomew County Courthouse renovation, 1998
Charles J. Budd Architect, Columbus, IN

Burd, William..Fire Station No. 3, 1983
Wood & Burd, Columbus, IN   Fire Station No. 2, (at the airport), 2009
                                                  Transit Center, Mill Race Center, 2011

Chihuly, Dale (b.1941) *glass sculptor, artist*............"Yellow Neon Chandelier" and Persians", 1995*
Pilchuck Glass School, Stanwood, Washington   "Sun Garden Panels in Suspended Circle", 2007*

Chermayeff, Ivan (b.1932) *graphic artist*................murals at Southside Middle School, 1969*
New York, NY
Harvard University, Yale University School of Design

Copley Wolff Design Group *landscape architects*....The Commons playground and streetscape, 2011*
Boston, MA (Carol Wolff, Sean Sanger)

Curtis, Jack *landscape architect*..........................Irwin Union & Trust Office building, 1972*
Jack Curtis & Associates, Monroe, CT   Cummins Corporate Office Building, 1984*
                                                  Columbus Visitors Center addition & renovation, 1995*
                                                  Cummins Engine Plant addition, 1996*
                                                  J. Irwin Miller residence garden restoration*

Architects / Landscape Architects / Artists and their works in Columbus, Indiana

Architect / Landscape Architect / Artist — *Building / Project / Artwork*

CSO Architects, Inc...Cummins Child Development Center, 2001* (*association with* Carlos Jimenez)
Indianapolis, IN
Central Middle School, 2007* (*association with* Ralph Johnson, Perkin+Will)
Commons Office Building, 2008* (*collaboration with* KKA)
Jackson Street facades, 2009
3rd Street Parking Garage, 2009*
The Commons, 2011* (collaboration with KKA)
Commons Office Building expansion, 2012* (*collaboration with* KKA)
The Cole apartments, 2012*
Columbus East High School addition and renovation, 2012
Columbus North High School addition and renovation, 2012
Urban Elements apartments, 2014*

De Harak, Rudolph (1924-2002) *graphic artist*.................."Exploded Engine" sculpture, 1985*
New York, NY

Dessa, Kirk *sculptor*..."Eos", 2006*
San Francisco, CA

Dinkeloo, John (1918-1981)... *see Kevin Roche for projects*
Kevin Roche John Dinkeloo & Associates, Hamden, CT

Fisher and Spillman Architects...........................Foundation of Youth, Boys Club and Girls Club addition, 1965 (demolished)
Dallas, TX
Taylorsville branch bank, 1966

Fletcher, Norman (1917-2007)...Parkside Elementary School, 1960: addition, 1990*
The Architects Collaborative, Cambridge, MA
BCSC Administration Building, 1963*
Yale University, 1940
Four Season Retirement Center, 1967*
worked for Skidmore, Owing & Merrill (SOM), 1943-1944
worked for Saarinen, Swanson & Associates, 1944-1945

Force, David (b.1956)...St. Peter's Lutheran School, 2003
Force Design, Columbus, IN
ArvinMeritor Columbus Technical Center, 2003
Home Federal Bank: Washington Street Branch
301 Washington Street interior renovation, 2012*

Garrison, Truitt (b.1936)..Fodrea Elementary School, 1973*
Caudill Rowlett Scott (CRS), Houston, TX

Girard, Alexander (1907-1993)...Miller House, 1957*
Sante Fe, NM
Washington Street Storefront project, 1964*
301 Washington Street facade and interiors, 1972*
Cummins headquarters interiors

Giurgola, Romaldo (b.1920)...East High School, 1972*
Mitchell/Giurgola Architects, Philadelphia, PA
East High School Gym addition, 1998
Mitchell/Giurgola Architects, Rizzoli, 1983

Goldsmith, Myron (1918-1996)...The Republic, 1971*
Skidmore, Owings & Merrill (SOM), Chicago, IL
Illinois Institute of Technology, 1939
worked with Mies van der Rohe, 1946-1953
Myron Goldsmith: Buildings and Concepts, Rizzoli, 1987

Graham, Wyatt S....Columbus Regional Hospital expansion, 1992*
Robert A.M. Stern Architects, New York, NY
Executive Architect to coordinate downtown planning, 2001-2002

GSI Architects (Forum Architects)..........................The Republic Printing Center, 1997*
Cleveland, OH

Gwathmey, Charles (1938-2009)....................................Sycamore Place senior housing, 1982*
Gwathmey Siegel & Associates Architects, New York, NY
Pence Place family housing, 1984*
Harvard University Graduate School of Design
  visiting professor 1985
Yale University, *professor* 1983, 1991, 1999
Gwathmey Siegel: Buildings and Projects 1982-1992
  Rizzoli, 1993

Hardy, Hugh (b.1932)...Mt. Healthy Elementary School, 1972*
Hardy Holzman Pfeiffer & Associates (HHPA), New York, NY
Cummins Health Center (Cummins Occupational Health Assoc.), 1973*
HHPA: Building and Projects 1967-1992
  Rizzoli, 1992

Hellmuth, Obata + Kassabaum (HOK)................Foundation for Youth, 1998
St. Louis, MO
Cummins Technical Center renovation, 1999*

Hisaka, Don M....Bartholomew County Jail, 1990*
Don M. Hisaka Architects, Cleveland, OH

Hodgson, Isaac (1826-1909)...Bartholomew County Courthouse, 1974*
Indianapolis, IN
founding member of Indiana Chapter of American Institute of Architects (AIA)

IDS, Inc....First Presbyterian Church renovation

Jimenez, Carlos (b.1959)...Cummins Child Development Center, 2001*
Carlos Jimenez Studio, Houston, TX
Cummins Child Development Center addition, 2004*
Carlos Jimenez: Buildings, Princeton Architectural Press, 1996
Irwin Union Bank, West Hills Plaza branch, 2001*
Irwin Union Bank, Seymour branch, 2001

Johansen, Christian M. (b.1958)..................................... L. Frances Smith Elementary School addition, 1997*
Loeffler, Johansen, Bennett, Architects, New Canaan, CT

Johansen, John M. (1916-2012).......................................L. Frances Smith Elementary School, 1969*
John Johansen Architect, New Canaan, CT
L. Frances Smith Elementary School addition, 1997* (*design consultant*)
Harvard University Graduate School of Design, 1939
worked for Skidmore, Owings, Merrill, NY, 1948
"Harvard Five" (Marcel Breuer, Philip Johnson,
  John Johansen, Landis Goris, Eliot Noyes)
Yale University professor

Architects / Landscape Architects / Artists   and their works in Columbus, Indiana

Architect / Landscape Architect / Artist   *Building / Project / Artwork*

Johnson, Ralph .... Central Middle School, 2007*
   Perkins+Will, Chicago, IL
   Harvard University Graduate School of Design
   <u>Ralph Johnson Perkins & Will: Normative Modernism</u>
     l'Arca Edizioni, 1998

Johnson, William (b.1931) *landscape architect* .... Columbus Alley Walkway projects, 1998*
   Johnson, Johnson & Roy, Ann Arbor, MI (1961-1975)
   William J. Johnson Associates (1980-1992)
   Harvard University Graduate School of Design, MLA
   Executive Architect to coordinate downtown planning

Johnson, J. Seward Jr. (b.1930) *sculptor* .... "When I Was Your Age", 1989*
   Santa Monica, CA

Jones, Rees (b.1941) *golf course architect* .... Otter Creek Golf Course expansion, 1995*
   Rees Jones, Montclair, NJ
   Yale University, 1963
   Harvard University Graduate School of Design, MLA, 1964

Jones, Robert Trent (1906-2000) *golf course architect* .. Otter Creek Golf Course, 1964*
   Robert Trent Jones, Sr., Montclair, NJ

Joyner, Louis (b.1955) .... Kirr Marbach renovation, 1995 (Joyner & Marshall Architects)
   Louis Joyner Architect, Columbus, IN
                                   Kidscommons, 2005*
                                   Miller House and Garden security gates, 2010
                                   Indiana University Center for Art + Design interiors, 2011

Indiana, Robert *artist* .... "C" wall hanging, 1981*
   Brookline, MA

Kennon, Paul (1934-1990) .... Fodrea Elementary School, 1973*
   Caudill Rowlett Scott (CRS), Houston, TX   Irwin Union Bank, State Street branch, 1974*
   Cranbrook Academy of Art, 1957   AT&T Switching Center, 1978*
   worked for Eero Saarinen, 1957-1964   Streetscape, 1990*
   Executive Architect to coordinate downtown planning   Mill Race Connected Parks project, ("Gateway" projects) 1988-1990*
   <u>Architecture and you: how to experience and enjoy buildings</u>
     Watson-Guptill Publications, 1981

Kennon, Kevin (b.1958) .... Columbus Learning Center, 2007*
   Kohn Pederson Fox (KPF), New York, NY
   Kevin Kennon Architect, New York, NY
   <u>Kohn Pederson Fox: Architecture and Urbanism 1993-2002</u>
     Rizzoli, 2002
   <u>Architecture tailored_Kevin Kennon/U.S.A.</u>
     Design Documents Series 16, 2006

Kiley, Dan (1912-2004) *landscape architect* .... Irwin Union Bank, 1954*
   Dan Kiley, Landscape Architect, Charlotte, VT   Miller House Gardens, 1957*
   Harvard University Graduate School of Design, *student* 1938   Cosco Inc. Office Building, 1962*
   collaborated with Eero Saarinen   North Christian Church, 1964*
     including St. Louis arch competition, 1947   Otter Creek Country Club, 1964*
   <u>Dan Kiley Landscapes: The Poetry of Spa</u>   First Baptist Church, 1965*
     Rainey & Treib, ed., William Stout Publishers   W.D. Richards Elementary School, 1965*
                                                  Taylorsville branch bank, 1966
                                                  Cummins Technical Center, 1968*
                                                  Central Avenue (Haw Creek Boulevard)
                                                  Cummins Occupational Health Center, 1973*
                                                  Cummins Midrange Engine Plant, 1973*
                                                  State Street branch bank, 1974*

Kim, Susie (b.1948) .... Downtown Columbus "Entertainment District" master plan, 2007
   Koetter Kim & Associates, Boston, MA   Jackson Street Parking Garage, 2009*
   Harvard University Graduate School of Design   Commons Office Building, 2008* (*collaboration with* CSO)
   <u>Koetter Kim & Associates: Place/Time</u>, Rizzoli, 1997   The Commons, 2011* (*collaboration with* CSO)

Koster & Associates .... Hamilton Center Ice Arena, 1975
   Cleveland, OH

Koetter, Fred (b.1938) .... Downtown Columbus "Entertainment District" master plan, 2007
   Koetter Kim & Associates, Boston, MA   Jackson Street Parking Garage, 2009*
   Yale University, *dean of* School of Architecture, 1993-1998   Commons Office Building, 2008* (*collaboration with* CSO)
   <u>Koetter Kim & Associates: Place/Time</u>, Rizzoli, 1997   The Commons, 2011* (*collaboration with* CSO)
                                                  Commons Office Building expansion, 2012* (*collaboration with* CSO)

Lee, John M.Y. .... W.D. Richards Elementary School addition, 1997
   John Lee / Michael Timchula Architects, New York, NY

Leers, Andrea .... Lillian Schmitt Elementary School addition, 1991*
   Leers, Weinzapfel & Associates (LWA), Boston, MA   NorthSide Middle School addition, 1991*
   <u>Made To Measure: The Architecture of LWA</u>
     Princeton Architectural Press, 2011

Luckey, Tom (1940-2012) *artist, architect* .... Luckey Climber, 2011*
   Luckey LLC, East Haven, CT
   Yale University, School of Architecture, 1962

Marcheschi, Cork *sculptor* .... Neon Sculpture, 1998*
   San Francisco, CA

Meier, Richard (b.1934) .... Clifty Creek Elementary School, 1982*
   Richard Meier & Associates, New York, NY
   <u>Richard Meier Architect: 1964/1984</u>, Rizzoli, 1984

Mitchell, Ehrman (1924-2005) .... East High School, 1972*
   Mitchell/Giurgola Architects, Philadelphia, PA   East High School Gym addition, 1998
   <u>Mitchell/Giurgola Architects</u>, Rizzoli, 1983

Moore, Henry (1898-1986) *sculptor* .... "Large Arch", 1971
   Much Hadham, Hertfordshire, England

Architects / Landscape Architects / Artists and their works in Columbus, Indiana

Architect / Landscape Architect / Artist *Building / Project / Artwork*

Muller, Jean M. (1925-2005) *bridge engineer* .... Overpass Bridge, I-65, 1997
J. Muller International, Chicago, IL Second Street Bridge, 1999

Nivola, Constantino (1911-1988) *sculptor* .... "Horse" (removed, one located at BCSC Admin. Office)
Long Island, NY

Noyes, Eliot (1917-1977) .... Southside Elementary School, 1969*
Eliot Noyes Architect, New Canaan, CT
Harvard University Graduate School of Design, 1938
"Harvard Five" (Marcel Breuer, Philip Johnson,
 John Johansen, Landis Goris, Eliot Noyes)

Paris, James K (b.1940) .... Senior Center, renovation of Power House, 1976
Paris Bingham, Columbus, IN City Hall (*facilities architect*)
 Cleo Rogers Memorial Library addition, 1987*
 Home Federal and Savings Bank
 Bartholomew County Jail, 1990* (*consultant to* Don M. Hisaka)
 Fire Station No. 1 addition, 1990*

Parnum, Edward J. (1901-1993) .... Home Federal Savings Bank
Edward J. Parnum Architect, Ardmore, PA

Partenheimer, David .... Sandy Hook United Methodist Church
McGuire & Shook Architects, Indianapolis, IN

Pei, I. M. (b.1917) .... Cleo Rogers Memorial Library, 1969*
I.M. Pei & Associates, New York, NY
Harvard University Graduate School of Design, 1939
I.M. Pei: Complete Works, Rizzoli, 2008

Pelli, Cesar (b.1926) .... The Commons and Commons Mall (Gruen Associates), 1973
Pelli Clarke Pelli, New Haven, CT Advanced Manufacturing Center, 2011*
worked for Eero Saarinen
Yale University, *dean of* School of Architecture, 1977-1984
Cesar Pelli, John Paster, Whitney Library of Design, 1980
Cesar Pelli: Buildings and Projects 1965-1990. Rizzoli, 1990
Cesar Pelli: Selected and Current Works, Images Publishing, 1993

Polshek, James Stewart (b.1930) .... Mental Health Center (Quinco Consulting Center), 1972*
James Stewart Polshek Architect, New York, NY
Yale University, M. Arch 1955
Columbia University, *dean of* School of Architecture, 1972-1987
James Stewart Polshek: Context and Responsibility,
 Buildings and Projects 1957-1987, Rizzoli, 1988

Rand, Paul (1914-1996) *graphic artist* .... Cummins logo, 1962*
 Cummins *graphic consultant*, 1961-1996
 A Look At Modern Architecture, 1978, 1980, 1984, 1991
 Dancing "C"s, consultant to Columbus Visitors Center

Ratio Architects, Inc. .... Arvin Corporate Headquarters, renovation & addition, 1989*
Indianapolis, IN St. Bartholomew Roman Catholic Church, 2002*
Ratio Architects: Innovation and Contextualism Columbus Learning Center, 2006* (*associate architect with* KPF)
 l'Arca Edizioni, 2001 Mill Race Center, 2011* (*associate architect with* William Rawn)
 Advanced Manufacturing Center, 2011* (*associate architect with* Cesar Pelli)

Rawn, William L., III (b.1943) .... Fire Station No. 6, 1998*
William Rawn & Associates, Boston, MA Mill Race Center, 2011*
Yale College, Harvard Law, MIT (M. Arch)
William Rawn: Architecture for the Public Realm
 Edizioni Press, 2002

Risting, Steven R. (b.1956) .... St. Bartholomew Roman Catholic Church, 2002* (Ratio Architects)
CSO Architects, Indianapolis, IN Northside Middle School addition, 2000 (Ratio Architects) (not built)
Harvard University Graduate School of Design, 1985 Commons Office Building, 2008* (*collaboration with* KKA)
 (Fred Koetter, thesis advisor) Jackson Street facades, 2009
 3rd Street Parking Garage, 2009
 The Commons, 2011* (*collaboration with* KKA)
 Commons Office Building expansion, 2012* (*collaboration with* KKA)
 The Cole apartments, 2013*
 Urban Elements apartments, 2014*

Roche, Kevin (b.1922) .... Miller House, 1957* (*design associate with* Eero Saarinen)
Kevin Roche John Dinkeloo & Associates, Hamden, CT North Christian Church, 1964* (*with* Eero Saarinen)
worked for Eero Saarinen 1950-1961 Columbus Post Office, 1970*
 Irwin Union Bank & Trust Company Office Building (addition), 1972*
 Columbus (Cummins) Midrange Engine Plant, Walesboro, 1973*
 Cummins Corporate Office Building, 1984*
 Irwin Union Capital Corporation, 520 Washington Street renovation, 1989
 Columbus Area Visitors Center addition & renovation, 1995*
 Cummins Engine Plant addition, 1996*

Rose, Charles (b.1960) .... Bartholomew County Veterans Memorial, 1997*
Thompson & Rose Architects, Cambridge, MA
Charles Rose Architects
Harvard University Graduate School of Design
Site/Architecture: Thompsom and Rose Architects
 Michigan Architecture Papers, 1998
Charles Rose Architect, Princeton Architectural Press, 2006

Roth, Harold "Harry" .... CERAland Recreation Center, 1982*
Roth and Moore Architects, New Haven, CT
Yale University
worked with Eero Saarinen

RQAW, Corporation .... Bartholomew County Jail addition, 2008*
Indianapolis, IN

Architects / Landscape Architects / Artists and their works in Columbus, Indiana

Architect / Landscape Architect / Artist   *Building / Project / Artwork*

Saarinen, Eero (1910-1961) .... First Christian Church, 1942*
    Eliel and Eero Saarinen, Bloomfield Hills, MI   Irwin Union Bank, 1954*
    Eero Saarinen & Associates, Bloomfield Hills, MI, 1950-1961   Miller House, 1957*
    Yale University, 1934   North Christian Church, 1964*
    Cranbrook Academy of Art
    <u>Eero Saarinen</u>, Rupert Spade, Simon and Schuster, 1971
    <u>Eero Saarinen: An Architecture of Multiplicity</u>
        Antonio Roman, Princeton Architectural Press, 2003
    <u>Eero Saarinen 1910-1961, A Structural Expressionist</u>
        Pierluigi Serraino, Taschen, 2005
    <u>Eero Saarinen: shaping the future</u>, Phaidon, 2006
    <u>Eero Saarinen: Buildings from the Balthazar Korab Archive</u>
        W.W. Norton & Co., 2008
    <u>Miller House and Gardens</u>, Assouline, 2011

Saarinen, Eliel (1873-1950) .... First Christian Church, 1942*
    Eliel and Eero Saarinen, Bloomfield Hills, MI
    Founding Director of Cranbrook Academy of Art
    <u>Eliel Saarinen: Finnish-American architect and educator</u>
        Albert Christ-Janer, University of Chicago Press, 1948, 1979

Saitowitz, Stanley (b.1949)
    Stanley Saitowitz | Natoma Architects, San Francisco, CA .... Mill Race Park structures, 1992*
    <u>Stanley Saitowitz: Buildings & Projects</u>. Monacelli Press, 2005

Saylors, Jo (b.1932), *sculptor* .... "Crack the Whip" 1998*
    Jo Saylors, Ponca City, OK   "Puddles and Frogs", 1998*

Shirley, Michael .... Foundation for Youth, 1998
    Hellmuth, Obata + Kassabaum (HOK), Houston, TX

Skidmore, Owens and Merrill (SOM) .... Downtown Master Plan, 1968
    Chicago, IL   The Republic (Myron Goldsmith), 1971*
         Columbus City Hall (Edward Charles Basset, San Francisco, CA), 1981*
         Downtown Master Plan, 1983

Sparrell, Charles F. (1852-1934) .... William Ruddick House (Ruddick-Nugent House), 1884*
    Columbus, IN   Fehring Block (Irwin Financial, Cummins), 1885
    Massachusetts Institute of Technology (MIT)   Crump Theater, 1889*
         Prall House, 1891*
         Odd Fellows lodge building, 1891
         McKinley School (McKinley apartments), 1892*
         U.S. Post Office (Viewpoint Books), 1894
         Columbus City Hall, 1895*
         Maple Grove / Garfield School (Arvin, BCSC Admin. Building), 1896*

Stamberg Aferiet Architecture .... Clifty Creek Elementary School addition and renovation, 1997*
    New York, NY

Stern, Robert A. M. (b.1939) .... Columbus Regional Hospital expansion, 1992*
    Robert A,M. Stern Architects, New York, NY
    Yale University, 1965
    Yale University, *dean of* School of Architecture, 1999-present
    <u>Robert A. M. Stern: Buildings</u>. Monacelli Press, 1996
    <u>Robert A. M. Stern: Buildings and Projects 1993-1998</u>
        The Monacelli Press, 1998

Storrow Kinsella Associates .... Tipton Lake community pocket parks, 1986-1996
    Indianapolis, IN   Columbus "Gateway" projects, 1987-1995*
    Meg Storrow *worked with* Jack Curtis   Columbus Alley Walkway (600 block), 1994*
    John Kinsella *worked with* Eero Saarinen
        and Kevin Roche John Dinkeloo and Associcates

Taft Architects .... Hope Elementary School, 1989*
    Houston, TX

Taylor, Dean .... Fodrea Elementary School, 1973* (*associate architect to* CRS)
    Dean Taylor Architect, Columbus, IN   Asbury United Methodist Church
         Bartholomew County Historical Society Museum renovation, 1973
         Prall House renovation, 1986*

The Architects Collaborative (TAC) .... Parkside Elementary School, 1960*, 1990 addition
    Cambridge, MA 1945-1995   BCSC Administration Building, 1963*
         Four Season Retirement Center, 1967*

Thompson, Maryann .... Bartholomew County Veterans Memorial, 1997*
    Maryann Thompson Architects
    Harvard University Graduate School of Design
    <u>Site/Architecture: Thompsom and Rose Architects</u>
        Michigan Architecture Papers, 1998

Tinguely, Jean (1925-1991), *sculptor* .... "Chaos I", 1974
    Zurich, Switzerland

Torre, Susanna (b.1944) .... Fire Station No. 5, 1987*
    Wank Adams Slavin Associates, New York
    Susana Torre and Associates, New York
    Director of Cranbrook Academy of Art, 1994-1995
    <u>The Design Process</u>, Whitney Library of Design, 1989

Van Valkenburgh, Michael (b.1951) *landscape* .... Mill Race Connected Parks & Golf Course project, 1990
    Michael Van Valkenburgh Associates (MVVA), Cambridge, MA   Downtown Parking Lots, 1990
    Harvard University Graduate School of Architecture   Mill Race Park, 1992*
        Chair of department of Landscape Architecture, 1991-1996   Columbus Gateway Project, 1991-1993
    <u>MVVA: Reconstruction Urban Landscapes</u>   Bartholomew County Courthouse Square project, 1993
        Yale University Press, 2009   Bartholomew County Veterans Memorial, landscape, 1997*

Venet, Benar (b.1941) *sculptor* .... "2 Arc de 212.5", 1987 sculpture*
    Atelier Marioni, Vosges, France

Architects / Landscape Architects / Artists and their works in Columbus, Indiana

Architect / Landscape Architect / Artist *Building / Project / Artwork*

Venturi, Robert (b.1925).. Fire Station No. 4, 1968*
    Venturi & Rauch, Philadelphia, PA   Columbus Gateway Project, 1991-1993* (not built)
    Venturi Scott Brown & Associates (VSBA)
    worked with Eero Saarinen, 1951
    <u>Venturi, Rauch & Scott Brown: Buildings and Projects</u>
        Stanislaus von Moos, Rizzoli, 1987
    <u>Venturi Scott Brown & Associates 1986-1998</u>
        Stanislaus von Moos, The Monacelli Press, 1999

Warnecke, John Carl (1919-2012).............................. Mabel McDowell Elementary School, 1960*
    John Carl Warnecke Architect, San Francisco, CA
    Harvard University Graduate School of Design, 1942

Weese, Harry (1915-1998).. Columbus Village, 1953 - 1960
    Harry Weese & Associates, Chicago, IL   Bassett House, 1953
    Massachusetts Institute of Technology (MIT), 1936, 1938   Lauther House, 1953
    Yale University, 1936-1937   Boys Club and Girls Club, 1954 (demolished)
    Cranbrook Academy, 1938-1939   Lillian C. Schmitt Elementary School, 1957*
    worked for Skidmore, Owing & Merrill (SOM), 1940, 1947   Irwin Union Bank, Hope, IN branch, 1958*
    <u>The Architecture of Harry Weese</u>   Lincoln Center (Hamilton Center Ice Arena), 1958*
        Robert Brugeman, 2010   Bartholomew County Home for the Aged (Salvation Army), 1959
        Cummins Engine Company Plant One Expansion, 1960, 1965*
        Irwin Union Bank, State Street Branch and Shopping Center, 1961
        Irwin Union Bank, Eastbrook Plaza branch, 1961*
        Northside Junior High School (Middle School), 1961^
        Cosco, Inc. Office Building, 1962*
        Otter Creek Gold Course Clubhouse, 1964*
        Newlin House, 1954
        First Baptist Church, 1965*
        Cummins Engine Company Technical Center, 1968*

Weinzapfel, Jane (b.1943)..Lillian Schmitt Elementary School addition, 1991*
    Leers, Weinzapfel & Associates (LWA), Boston, MA   NorthSide Middle School addition, 1991*
    <u>Made To Measure: The Architecture of LWA</u>   *
        Princeton Architectural Press, 2011

Wiley, William T. (b.1937), *artist*.."History-Mystery" mural, Columbus City Hall, 1984*
    San Francisco, CA (born Bedford, Indiana)

Williams, Todd (b.1958)..The Commons Mall renovations and storefronts, 1989-1993
    Todd Williams & Associates, Columbus, IN   IMA-Columbus Gallery & Gift Shop at The Commons, 1993
    worked with Cesar Pelli, 1983   The Republic renovations, 1997*
        Columbus Visitors Center addition & renov., 1995* (*association with* KRJDA)
        B.C. Veterans Memorial, 1997* (*site architect for* Thompson & Rose)
        West Hills Plaza branch bank, 2001* (*association with* Carlos Jimenez)
        Creekview branch bank, 2006* (*associate with* Deborah Berke)
        Jackson Street Parking garage, 2009* (*association with* Koetter Kim)
        Irwin Union Office Building renovations, 2012* (*collaboration with* KRJDA)
        Cummins Parking Garage, 2012* (*association with* StructurePoint, KRJDA)

Modern Architecture & Public Art in Columbus, Indiana — Listed alphabetically with location

Modern Buildings and Public Art listed alphabetically
Original Architect or Artist listed, with original date completed (see TIMELINE or project narrative for additions)
Location is in relationship to downtown, see project narrative for address.

Modern Buildings

Building	Architect	Location	Page
301 Washington St. facade & interiors, 1972	Alexander Girard	Downtown	72
Advanced Manufacturing Center, 2011	Cesar Pelli	North	160
AT&T Switching Center, 1978	Paul Kennon (CRS)	Downtown	92
Bartholomew County Jail, 1990	Don M. Hisaka	Downtown	112
Bartholomew County Public Library, 1969	I.M. Pei	Downtown	62
BCSC Administration Building, 1963	Norman Fletcher (TAC)	Near North	44
Breeden Realtors Office Building, 1995	Thomas Beeby (HBA)	Downtown	120
Central Middle School, 2007	Ralph Johnson (P+W)	Downtown	150
CERAland Recreation Center, 1982	Harry Roth	Far East	96
Clifty Creek Elementary School, 1982	Richard Meier	East	98
The Cole apartments, 2012	Steven Risting (CSO)	Downtown	156
Columbus East High School, 1972	Romaldo Giurgola (MGA)	East	74
Columbus "Gateway" projects	Kennon/Venturi	West	126
Columbus City Hall, 1981	Edward C. Bassett (SOM)	Downtown	94
Columbus Learning Center, 2006	Kevin Kennon (KPF)	North	146
Columbus Regional Hospital, 1992	Robert A.M. Stern	Northeast	116
The Commons, 2011	Koetter Kim/CSO	Downtown	162
Commons Office Building, 2009	CSO/Koetter Kim	Downtown	154
Cosco Inc. Office Building, 1962	Harry Weese	East	40
Creekview branch bank, 2006	Deborah Berke	East	148
Cummins Child Development Center, 2001	Carlos Jimenez	East	138
Cummins Columbus Engine Plant addition, 1996	Kevin Roche	East	124
Cummins Columbus Midrange Engine Plant, 1973	Kevin Roche	South	86
Cummins Corporate Office Building, 1983	Kevin Roche	Downtown	102
Cummins Health Center, 1973	Hugh Hardy (HHPA)	East	84
Cummins Parking Garage, 2011	Kevin Roche	Downtown	164
Cummins Technical Center, 1968	Harry Weese	East	60
Eastbrook Plaza branch bank, 1961	Harry Weese	Northeast	38
Fire Station No. 1, 1941	Leighton Bowers	Downtown	210
Fire Station No. 4, 1968	Robert Venturi	Northeast	58
Fire Station No. 5, 1987	Susana Torre	West	106
Fire Station No. 6, 1998	William Rawn	South	132
First Baptist Church, 1965	Harry Weese	Northeast	50
First Christian Church, 1942	Eliel Saarinen	Downtown	20
Fodrea Community School, 1973	Paul Kennon (CRS)	East	88
Four Seasons Retirement Center, 1967	Norman Fletcher (TAC)	Northeast	54
Freedom Park, 2006		North	42
"Friendship Way" Alley Walkway Project, 1998	William Johnson	Downtown	134
Hamilton Center Ice Arena, 1958	Harry Weese	Northeast	30
Hope branch bank, 1958	Harry Weese	Hope, IN	32
Hope Elementary School, 1989	Taft Architects	Hope, IN	110
Hope Library, 1998	Deborah Berke	Hope, IN	134
I-65 Overpass Bridge, 1997	Jean Muller	West	126
Irwin Union Bank, 1954	Eero Saarinen	Downtown	22
Irwin Office Building, 1972	Kevin Roche	Downtown	82
Jackson Street Parking Garage, 2009	Koetter Kim	Downtown	152
Kidscommons, 2005	Louis Joyner	Downtown	210
Lincoln Elementary School, 1967	Gunnar Birkerts	Downtown	56
Luckey Climber, 2011	Tom Luckey	Downtown	194
Mabel McDowell Adult Education Center, 1960	John Carl Warnecke	East	34
Mental Health Center, 1972	James S. Polshek	Northeast	80
Mill Race Center, 2011	William Rawn	Near West	158
Mill Race Park, 1992	Michael Van Valkenburgh	Near West	118
Miller House and Garden, 1957	Eero Saarinen	Near North	24
Mt. Healthy Elementary School, 1972	Hugh Hardy (HHPA)	Southwest	76
North Christian Church, 1964	Eero Saarinen	Near North	46
Northside Middle School, 1961	Harry Weese	Near North	36
Otter Creek Clubhouse and Golf Course, 1965	Harry Weese	Far East	48

Modern Architecture & Public Art in Columbus, Indiana

Listed alphabetically with location

Modern Buildings

Building	Architect	Location	Page
Par 3 Golf Course Clubhouse, 1972	Bruce Adams	Northeast	78
Parkside Elementary School, 1962	Norman Fletcher	North	42
Pence Place apartments, 1984	Charles Gwathmey (GSA)	East	104
U.S. **Post Office** - Columbus, 1970	Kevin Roche	Downtown	68
The **Republic**, 1971	Myron Goldsmith (SOM)	Downtown	70
The **Republic Printing Center**, 1998	GSI (Forum)	Southwest	130
W.D. **Richards Elementary School**, 1965	Edwards L. Barnes	Northeast	52
Salvation Army Corps Community Center, 1959	Harry Weese	East	
Lillian C. **Schmitt Elementary School**, 1957	Harry Weese	Near North	28
Second Street Bridge, 1999	Jean Muller	Downtown	126
L. Frances **Smith Elementary School**, 1969	John Johansen	Northeast	64
Southside Elementary School, 1969	Eliot Noyes	South	66
St. Bartholomew Roman Catholic Church, 2002	Steven Risting (Ratio)	Near North	144
St. Paul's Episcopal Church renovation, 2002	Thomas Beeby (HBBA)	Near North	142
St. Peter's Lutheran Church, 1988	Gunnar Birkerts	Downtown	108
State Street branch bank, 1974	Paul Kennon (CRS)	East	90
Streetscape, 1990	Paul Kennon (CRS)	Downtown	114
Sycamore Place, 1982	Charles Gwathmey (GSA)	East	100
Third Street Parking Garage, 2009	Steven Risting (CSO)	Downtown	156
Urban Elements apartments, 2014	Steven Risting (CSO)	Downtown	164
Columbus Area **Visitor Center addition**, 1995	Kevin Roche	Downtown	122
Bartholomew County **Veterans Memorial**, 1997	Thompson and Rose	Downtown	128
West Hill Plaza branch bank, 2001	Carlos Jimenez	West	140

Public Art

Work	Artist / Sculptor	Location	Page
"2 Arcs de 212.5", 1987	Bernar Venet	Downtown	180
"Ancestral Way", 2006	Robert Pulley	Downtown	182
"Birds of Fire", 1979 (removed 2012)	Ted Sitting Crow Garner	Downtown	176
Boy on a Dolphin, 1930+	unknown	Downtown	168
Boy with Duck, 1930+	unknown	Downtown	168
Bronze Cummins Engine		Downtown	186
"C" wall hanging, 1981	Robert Indiana	Downtown	184
"Celebration", 1998	Gary Price	East	188
"Chaos I", 1974	Jean Tinguely	Downtown	172
City Hall murals	various artists	Downtown	184
"Crack the Whip" 1998	Jo Saylors	Downtown	178
"Daquqi", 1988	Peter Lunderg	Downtown	182
"Discovery", 2007	Kusser Granitwerks	North	190
"Elephant", 1932	Golden Foundry	Downtown	168
"Eos", 2006	Dessa Kirk	Downtown	176
"Exploded Engine"	Rudolph de Harak	Downtown	186
Freedom Field sculptures, 2006		North	192
"Halcyon", 2011	Todd Frahm	Northeast	188
"Generations", 2002	Betty Boyle	Downtown	184
Hamilton Center sculpture, 2000	North High School	Northeast	192
"History-Mystery", 1984	William T. Wiley	Downtown	184
"Iris", 1997	Scott Westphal	Downtown	182
"Jacobs Ladder", 2006	Bernie Carrefio	Downtown	180
"Large Arch", 1971	Henry Moore	Downtown	170
Luckey Climber, 2011	Tom Luckey	Downtown	194
Material Column, Cummins Engine		Downtown	186
"Persians", 1995	Dale Chihuly	Downtown	174
"Puddles and Frog Pond", 1998	Jo Saylors	East	178
"Self-Made Man", 2015	Bobbie Carlye	North	190
"Skopos", 1979	Rick Bauer	Near West	178
"Summer Storm", 2006 (removed 2012)	Michael Helbing	Downtown	180
"Sun Garden" panels in suspended circle, 2007	Dale Chihuly	North	174
"The Family", 1964	Harris Barron	North	188
"Transformation", 2010	Howard Meehan	North	190
"When I Was Your Age", 1989	J. Seward Johnson, Jr.	South	192
"Yellow Neon Chandelier", 1995	Dale Chihuly	Downtown	174
"Yellowwood Coral", 2006	Lucy Slivinski	East	192

Columbus, Indiana Contractors contribution to excellence

While Columbus is know for its modern architecture by national and internationally renowned architects, many of these meticulously detailed buildings are realized by the craftsmanship and management of local construction firms working with these prominent architects. There are four major construction companies that have been a part of constructing many of these masterpieces.

Dunlap & Company
General Contractor, Mechanical Contractor, Masonry

1957	Lillian C. Schmitt Elementary School (Harry Weese)
1967	Lincoln Elementary School (Gunnar Birkerts)
1971	The Republic (SOM)
1969	Cleo Rogers Memorial Library (I.M. Pei)
1981	City Hall (SOM) *(masonry)*
1992	Columbus Regional Hospital expansion (Robert Stern)
1995	Columbus Visitors Center (Kevin Roche)
1995	Breeden Realty Office Building (Thomas Beeby)
1997	The Republic Printing Center (GSI)
1997	Veteran's Memorial (Thompson Rose)
1998	Fire Station No. 6 (Rawn)
1998	Foundation for Youth (HOK)
2002	St. Bartholomew Roman Catholic Church (Steven Risting / Ratio)
2007	Central Middle School (Ralph Johnson / Perkins+Will / CSO)
2011	The Commons (Koetter Kim / CSO)

Force Construction Company, Inc.
General Contractor, Design/Build (Force Design, Inc.)

1988	St. Peter's Lutheran Church (Gunnar Birkerts)
1992	Mill Race Park Tower (Stanley Saitowitz)
2003	ArvinMeritor Columbus Technical Center
2003	St. Peter's Lutheran School (David Force)
2006	Creekview branch bank (Deborah Berke)
2012	301 Washington Street interior renovation (David Force)

Repp & Mundt
General Contractor, Restoration, Masonry

1960	Mabel McDowell Elementary School (John Carl Warnecke)
1961	Eastbrook branch bank (Harry Weese)
1961	State Street branch bank and Shopping Center (Harry Weese)
1961	Northside Middle School (Harry Weese)
1965	First Baptist Church (Harry Weese)
1973	Cummins Occupational Health Association (Polshek)
1984	Cerealine Building restoration (Kevin Roche)
1987	Fire Station No. 5 (Susana Torre)
1989	Hope Elementary School (Taft) *(masonry)*
1964	North Christian Church (Eero Saarinen)
1995	Columbus Visitors Center (Kevin Roche)
1996	Cummins Plant One Addition (Kevin Roche)
1998	Hope Library (Deborah Berke)
2005	Columbus Learning Center (Kevin Kennon / KPF) *(masonry)*

Taylor Bros. Construction Co., Inc.
General Contractor, Construction Manager, Owner's Representative

1957	Miller House (Eero Saarinen)
1958	Lincoln Center (Hamilton Center) (Harry Weese)
1961	Eastbrook branch bank (Harry Weese)
1964	Newlin Residence (Harry Weese)
1970	Columbus Post Office (Kevin Roche)
1972	Irwin Bank Office Building Addition (Kevin Roche)
1996	Cummins Plant One Addition (Kevin Roche)
2001	Cummins Child Care Center (Carlos Jimenez)
2005	Columbus Learning Center (Kevin Kennon / KPF)
2011	Mill Race Center (Rawn)
2011	Advanced Manufacturing Center (Pelli)
2011	The Commons (Koetter Kim / CSO) *(owner's representative)*

Columbus, Indiana

Map (districts)

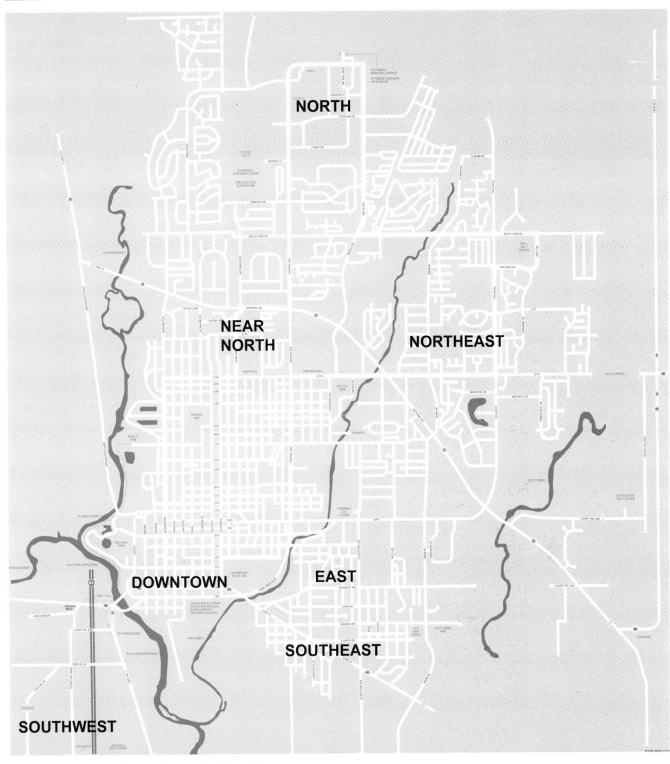

A detailed Columbus Indiana Architectural Tour Map is available at the Columbus Area Visitors Center

For more information about Columbus Indiana and its architectural tours, contact or visit the
Columbus Area Visitors Center:
506 Fifth Street, Columbus, Indiana 47201
800.468.6564 / 812.378.2622
info@columbus.in.us • www.columbus.in.us

columbusindiana
visitorscenter

unexpected.**unforgettable.**

www.columbus.in.us

unexpected.**unforgettable.**

www.columbus.in.us

ACKNOWLEDGMENTS:

I want to thank the Columbus Area Visitors Center for their endorsement and support of this project, especially Lynn Lucas, the executive director, the staff, and the board of directors. Their book, <u>Columbus, Indiana: A Look At Architecture</u>, has been the most comprehensive documentation of the remarkable architecture and art of Columbus, Indiana since its first edition in 1974. It has been a privilege to recreate this book, including updating the layout, revising the text and photographing the significant architecture and public art. We have tried to update and correct previous editions as accurately as possible. I have been fortunate to have become a part of this unique community through the architectural projects that I have been associated with, planning an American Institute of Architects Committee on Design conference, and this book project.

Many people have assisted me in reviewing and commenting on the book revisions, including Ricky Berkey, Bradley Brooks, Jan Forbes, Louis Joyner, Will Miller, Karen Shroder, Tom Vujovich and others that I apologize for not mentioning. The Columbus Indiana Architectural Archives has been an invaluable resource for confirming information and discovering original design intentions. I especially want to thank my wife, Carol, for her editing, patience and support, as I spent many hours photographing, researching and laying out this project, while still practicing full time as an architect.
Steven R. Risting
Indianapolis, 2012

CREDITS:

Layout & Editing:	Steven R. Risting
Photography: (except as noted)	Steven R. Risting
Contributing Photographers:	Jennifer Risting cover, p. 212 *courtesy of* Indianapolis Museum of Art Miller House & Gardens, p. 12, 22-24 Susan Fleck Commons & Luckey Climber, p. 167 bottom, 174-175
Plans & Renderings:	Courtesy of the architects or the Columbus Indiana Architectural Archives
Printing:	Pentzer Printing
Editors:	Lynn Lucas Tom Vujovich